BELGIUM
AND
LUXEMBOURG

Nina Nelson

BELGIUM
AND
LUXEMBOURG

B. T. Batsford Ltd   London and Sydney

To James Holloway

First published 1975
© Nina Nelson 1975

Made and printed in Great Britain by
Cox & Wyman Ltd., London, Fakenham and Reading
for the publishers B. T. Batsford Ltd
4 Fitzhardinge Street, London W1
and 23 Cross Street, Brookvale, NSW 2100, Australia

ISBN 0 7134 2994 1

Contents

Illustrations

Acknowledgments

Many Belgian friends made this book possible, in particular Pierre Claus, the director of the Belgium National Tourist Office in London, who with his usual enthusiasm, not only had many helpful suggestions but smoothed my path. Virginia Spruyt, the director of the same office in Amsterdam, accompanied me on several jaunts and introduced me to carnivals. Her knowledge of her own country is exceptional. Françoise de Saligny, who opened my eyes to facets of Belgian painting which would otherwise have escaped me. James Holloway, who is English but knows and loves Belgium so well that he is 'at home' in either country. Indeed it was his idea that I should write this book.

In Belgium itself I owe special thanks to Mr Arthur Haulot who extended to me all possible help through his excellent Tourist Organisation. He is also chairman of the European Travel Commission and, having been through the horrors of concentration camps during the last World War, is anxious that the ordinary man and woman in every country should meet and learn to understand their opposite numbers.

I am equally grateful to Mr Arthur Haulot's wonderful team in Brussels; Mr Jean Gyory, Press and Public Relations Officer, and his able assistant Cecile Pierarad who arranged my itinerary. Also Gilbert Sadaune who knows his way round the network of new highways, as well as country roads.

My thanks to Roland Annoot, chief of West Flanders Tourism who directs his work from the charming town of Bruges and was tireless in his efforts to help; to Robert Van Loo of the same town. My thanks are also due to Yvonne Fontinoy, Marie Claire Provis, Madame Zimmer van Oort, Marie Jeanne Lambot, Luc Verwerft, Georges Kinart, Robert Quintens, Jan Breyne, and last, but by no means least, M Baudoux, all of whom infected me with their enthusiasm for their 'parishes'.

In Luxembourg I wish to express my deep gratitude to Mr Georges Hausemer, Director of the Luxembourg National Tourist Office, for enabling me to visit so much of his delightful country with which I immediately fell in love. Also to Teddy Pescatore, the director in the London office who gave unstinted help in arranging my trip and was a fund of knowledge. Back in Luxembourg I would like to thank Camille Klein, Ray George and John Barter of Radio Luxembourg. Sepp Simon, Professor at the Lycée Classique, Echternach, put his unrivalled knowledge of the historical background of the town at my disposal.

Finally I would like to thank Marie Chitty who, despite her busy life, always helps me reach my deadline!

The Author and Publishers are grateful to the following for supplying photographs that appear in the book: Simone Annout for plates 5 and 11; Douglas Dickins for plates 1, 10 and 13; James Holloway for plates 6, 15 and 16; and the Institut Belge d'Information et de Documentation for plates 3 and 9. Plates 2, 4, 7, 14, 17–22 were taken by the Author.

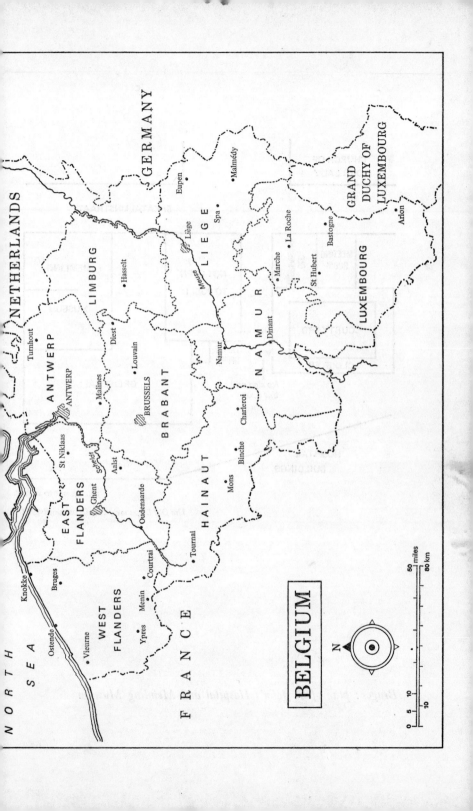

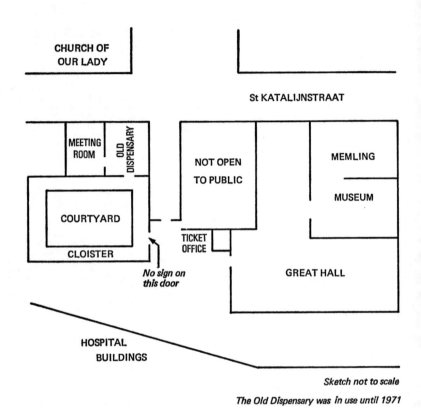

CHURCH OF
OUR LADY

St KATALIJNSTRAAT

MEETING
ROOM

OLD DISPENSARY

NOT OPEN
TO PUBLIC

MEMLING

MUSEUM

COURTYARD

CLOISTER

TICKET
OFFICE

GREAT HALL

*No sign on
this door*

HOSPITAL
BUILDINGS

Sketch not to scale

The Old Dispensary was in use until 1971

Bruges: plan of St John's Hospital and Memling Museum

Belgium

1. History and Culture

Belgian towns are so neatly packed, the scenery so varied that one is never conscious of lack of space. Scarcely larger than Wales, and one of Europe's smallest countries, Belgium lies between France, Germany, Luxembourg and Holland. Nowhere are her frontiers as much as 200 miles apart. Yet miraculously she does not feel hemmed in for her open coastline stretches some 40 miles – from the Dutch frontier to the French. From the south east the land gradually slopes down to the North Sea and is enriched and drained by the Scheldt and the Meuse rivers and the lacework of their various tributaries, the most important of the latter being the Sambre.

The triangular section south of the Sambre-Meuse waters is made up of extensive plateaux trenched by ravines and narrow valleys. Moor and marshland merge into the attractively wooded Ardennes. Here you might be alone in the silence of a Canadian forest. There is always the feeling that you can get away from it all in Belgium although over nine million people live within its 11,755 square miles.

The country to the north, known as the Campine, was a barren sandy area at one time but generations of hardy peasantry have drawn crops from the arid earth by patiently nursing, tilling and heavily manuring the soil until, by the second half of the nineteenth century, over 270,000 acres had been won over by effective cultivation. Belgium's wealth has been produced by such perseverance as this and often also by astonishing far-sightedness like that shown by Leopold II when he acquired the Congo, 80 times larger than Belgium herself. Mineral riches include the coal and iron industries of Charleroi and Liège, Flemish textiles are second to none and navigation in the Scheldt has raised the status of Antwerp to that of one of the world's greatest commercial ports. Brussels, among her many accolades, is now capital of the EEC and continues to grow as a diplomatic and financial centre, while the art centres of Bruges and Ghent cater for more visitors each year.

Motorists often refer jokingly to Belgium as a place to drive through en route to somewhere else and it is just because of its strategic position as the cross roads of Europe that, over the centuries, it has always been a tempting prize for warring nations. History has left its mark on every town.

Tugs-of-war in the past between the French, Spanish, Austrians and the Dutch have made a deep impression on the character of the Belgian people and their resilience under adversity is remarkable. Occupation by the Germans during the last two World Wars only served to strengthen their skills in circumventing alien laws and regulations, not to mention food rationing. It is said that allied aircraft always knew when they were over Belgium by the appetizing smell of crisp potato chips, the Belgians' beloved *frites*. However scarce or dull the food during the German occupation one thing was certain in Belgium: it was cooked superbly. Indeed when the Belgian protects his own interests fiercely it is called 'Defending his beefsteak'.

The Belgian is courteous, formal and polite. His family is closely knit and his religion almost universally Roman Catholic. He enjoys his profession or work and tackles it with zeal; with the same zeal he enjoys his leisure hours and festivals. The latter are part of every Belgian's life and there are so many during the year that visitors often come upon them by chance. The most famous one is probably at Bruges which has its annual 'Procession of the Holy Blood' on Ascension Day. Other well known ones are the 'Procession of the Penitents' at Furnes and the 'Blessing of the Sea' at Blankenberge. Ghent has a quinquennial flower show, Eupen and Malmedy have carnivals just before Lent and the Carnival of the Gilles at Binche is so riotous that many linguists believe that the English word 'binge' comes from it.

Actually we use several words in every-day conversation which are Belgian. The town of Duffel, famous for its factory, gave its name to sturdy bags and coats carried or worn by most soldiers and sailors even today. Spa, the pioneer watering place frequented by royalty during the eighteenth century, has become the word that denotes any place with curative springs; and who has not heard of – or eaten – Brussel sprouts?

Nowhere will you find the shopping pavements as clean as in Belgium. Each shopkeeper is responsible for the frontage outside his store and early every weekday morning the sidewalks are awash with water and suds as brooms are wielded vigorously back and forth and foaming water vanishes down the gutters. The narrowness of older houses often astonishes visitors, especially as the width will only equal a quarter of the back-to-front depth. It is even more amazing when this happens in the countryside where there is plenty of room and no house on either side. As in Holland where such houses are similar, there is a very good reason. At the turn of the century householders were taxed on the width of their frontage but not on the depth of their homes, which means you will find houses where each floor consists of three or four rooms leading out of one another from the front of the house to the back. Therefore there can only be windows in the front and back rooms but both the Dutch and the Belgians have learnt how to furnish their rooms with the aid of mirrors and cleverly spaced furniture so that this is not immediately apparent.

The Belgians are passionately fond of cycling. Every boy dreams of winning a championship and those who do are as famous as film stars. Another great pastime is *pelote,* a mixture of tennis and handball, which is played on squares and wide streets with as much dedication as the British give to cricket.

Despite the fact that supermarkets, with acres of parking space, and self-service stores have come to stay, the little retailer still exists and it is often possible to buy things quite late at night.

One of the main features of Belgian shopping is still the street market with its fresh fruit and vegetables attractively and colourfully displayed. Small family businesses prosper but there is little extravagance and money is saved 'for a rainy day'. Hire purchase is frowned upon but casinos flourish!

The Belgian is international in his thinking and a good linguist but, as with most nations, he has a pressing problem at home. In the same way as Canadians are divided into English- and French-speaking cities with bitter rivalries, so the Belgian has Flemish- and French-speaking provinces. Both Fleming and Walloon are subjects of King Baudouin who is not King of Wallonia or Flanders but King of the Belgians. The Fleming is usually fair-haired, thick set and obstinate, says the Walloon, whereas the Fleming describes the Walloon as smaller, darker and volatile. Perhaps the difference is explained in a couple of jokes. Two road work parties set up little wooden huts on either side of the road. The Walloons put up a sign saying 'We speak French here'. The Flemish in retort put up a notice reading 'We work here'. One day driving along a rough pavé road my taxi driver, a Walloon, turned around and said with a grin, 'We are driving over the hard heads of the Flemish'. This situation makes for friction and there is much fun had by both sides berating each other but, again as in the case of the Canadians, let someone from outside attack either Flemings or Walloons and both are at his throat. It is apparent that beneath the grumbling and insults there is a family unity that nothing outside can break.

Officially there has been a movement in some provinces to adopt Flemish, a tongue similar to the Dutch language, for official usage although the rest of the country conducts its affairs in French. In order to understand all this a thumbnail sketch of Belgian history may help.

To go back to the days when Roman legions marched towards the North Sea, Caesar himself is said to have remarked that of those who stood in their path – Belgians, Gauls and Aquitanians – 'from all these peoples the Belgians are the most courageous'.

When the Romans withdrew during the fifth century the

1 *Grand' Place, Brussels*

2 *Part of the Atomium on the outskirts of Brussels*

Frankish kingdom of the Merovingian Kings stretched from Tournai to the Pyrenees. The dynasty weakened and Pope Leo III made Charlemagne Emperor with rule extending from Jutland to Naples and from the Ebro to the Oder. After his death the Treaty of Verdun cut his Kingdom into three parts which were ruled by his three grandsons. A boundary along the Scheldt separated Flanders from Belgium's southern (Wallonia) provinces. So Flanders was strengthened and Wallonia weakened.

In the northern half of the country Baudouin Iron Arm became the first Count of Flanders. During this period the first Anglo-Flemish bond was forged when Baudouin's son, Baudouin the Bald, married a daughter of King Alfred the Great of England. South of the Scheldt, Flanders expanded into France and the Netherlands. Later the southern kingdom ran into trouble and quarrelling with the Papacy broke out. When the famous Godefroy de Bouillon, together with other knights and their followers, went to the Middle East on the First Crusade their feudal domains were left to the mercy of the masterful Prince-Bishops of Liège.

The Counts of Flanders grew less important with the emergence of the new commercial cities which broke away from the old feudal system and demanded their own privileges. They set up their own administration and universities, even their own defences. Trade, regulated by guilds, increased and brought such wealth that merchants could afford to embellish their towns with impressive buildings. Splendid new abbeys and castles were built and rich endowments were bequeathed to those already in existence. Riches were brought to Ghent and Ypres by the sale of fine cloth made there. Liège had deposits of iron and became well known for its arms production.

Bruges, with its port on the Zwin, grew to be the central clearing house of Europe's trade and France decided it was time to step in to stem this growth. A battle was fought near Courtrai which became known as the 'Battle of the Golden Spurs'. The French were defeated and the victors picked up hundreds of golden spurs from the battlefield and suspended them as trophies from the roofing of the Church of Our Lady. Later in 1382 the French retrieved these after the battle of Westrozebeke and to-day you will find only one authentic golden spur in the town museum.

The most famous of the Dukes of Burgundy was Philip the Good who brought Belgium to a pinnacle of culture. It was the time of the Van Eycks and Hans Memling, architects such as Jan van Ruysbroeck and Mathieu de Layens and the sculptors Claus Sluter and the Borremans. Not only the arts were in ascendancy; Philip allied himself with Henry v of England, gained Hainaut, Namur and Luxembourg and was proclaimed heir to the Duchies of Brabant, Limburg and Antwerp. Ghent and Bruges grew in splendour. Indeed the latter was at the height of its prosperity, the northern counterpart of Venice, and its Bourse regulated the rate of exchange in Europe.

On the day of Philip the Good's marriage to Isabel of Portugal, 10 January 1429, he founded the Order of the Golden Fleece. The number of knights was limited to 24, exclusive of the Grand Master, the King. Four reasons have been suggested for the name. Perhaps the scriptural story of Gideon, the staple trade of Flanders in wool, the golden hair of Marie de Rambrugge (the king's former mistress) or, probably the most likely, the classical myth of Jason and the Argonauts' voyage to find the golden fleece. Whatever the reason the historian Motley asks: 'What could be more practical and more devout than the conception? Did not the Lamb of God, suspended at each knight's heart, symbolize at once the woollen fabrics to which so much of Flemish wealth and Burgundian power was owing, and the gentle humility of Christ which was ever to characterize the order?' The members were to be *'gentilshommes de nom et d'armes et sans reproche'*, not knights of any other order, and vowed to join their sovereign in the defence of the Catholic faith, the protection of the Holy Church, and the upholding of virtue and good morals. The sovereign undertook to consult the knights before embarking on a war; all disputes between the knights were to be settled by the Order, at meetings the deeds of each knight were held in review and punishments and admonitions were dealt out to offenders; to this the sovereign was expressly subject.

During the sixteenth century the Order frequently acted as a consultative body in the state and privy councils to decide what steps should be taken in a crisis. One instance was the revolt of Ghent and in 1562 Margaret of Parma, the regent, asked the Order to debate the dangerous condition of the provinces. The knights were present at the abdication of Charles Quint in the Great Hall at Brussels in 1555. Earlier, by the marriage of Mary, daughter of Charles the Bold of Burgundy, to Maximilian, Archduke of Austria, the Grand Mastership of the Order came to the house of Hapsburg. It passed, with the Netherlands provinces, to Spain in 1504 on the accession of Phillip, Maximilian's son, to Castile.

The insignia itself is a most attractive one for, suspended from the collar beneath various ribbons, hangs a tiny, limp golden ram with curved horns.

Of the famous people that Belgium has produced, the artists are outstanding. With what drollness Breughel the Elder depicts country life. The onlooker cannot but smile. During Breughel's life story-telling in paintings was one of the main ways of communicating ideas. A nation whose homeland is used constantly as a cockpit and which knows the necessity of not speaking openly about religion or politics, turns to symbols for a rough philosophy and robust laughter relieves pent-up feelings.

Who can look at such paintings as 'The Wedding Feast', 'The Peasant Dance' or 'Children's Games' without a grin? Their very liveliness cheers the day and one can sense the summer torpor, the sunlit drowsy air and the heat haze in 'The Harvesters in Summer'. You can feel the lethargy of the farm hands as they lazily cut the hay.

How very different is the sophisticated Rubens from Breughel the Elder. He was not only one of the world's greatest artists but one of the most famous scholars of his day, a traveller and a diplomat. His teacher Adam Van Noort also taught Jordaens. Rubens' own pupils included Van Dyck, Van den Hoech and the great

Van Oost of Bruges. During Rubens' lifetime well known de-
picters of flowers, animals and still life came to the fore, as did
an entire school of famed engravers. It was an age of prosperity
which can be judged by the vigorous but plump and contented
figures in portraits. Rubens' luxurious display of white and rosy
flesh on well-nourished bodies may not appeal today but the pale
silkiness of blonde tresses, the matchless folds and colours of bro-
cades and canopies, the Venetian stairways, temples, ships and
animals are real enough. It is said there is only one Rubens in
Belgium as there is only one Shakespeare in England.

In 1556 Charles Quint's son Philip II inherited Belgium and
Holland, dealt harshly with religious troubles and had so-called
'heretics' executed. He ordered the arrest and execution of the
Counts of Egmont and Hoorn, who are remembered as heroes to
this day. Holland, of Protestant persuasion, became independent
but Belgium, with its Catholic leanings, preferred to remain
under the Spanish yoke. The Treaty of Utrecht brought Belgium under Austrian rule again which lasted throughout the
remainder of the eighteenth century. By the time Napoleon's star
had arisen, Austria had ceded her Belgian provinces to France –
much to English displeasure. Catholicism became the state religion once more but Napoleon was not popular and, by the time
of the Battle of Waterloo, French rule was meeting much resistance with Liège appearing to be the only loyal province. Many
Belgian troops fought alongside the British during the famous
battle. Although the French have a natural bias towards Napoleon the English received an accolade from one great French-
man, Victor Hugo himself, when he praised Wellington's men
later in *Les Miserables*: 'What is truly admirable in the battle
of Waterloo is England, English firmness, English resolution,
English blood; the superb thing which England had there – may
it not displease her – is herself'.

The Congress of Vienna in 1815 formed Belgium and Holland
into the Kingdom of the Netherlands under William of Orange,
but rioting soon broke out in Brussels and this flared like wildfire
into real revolution, with the result that the Dutch were driven

out and a provisional Belgian government was set up. France and Britain encouraged Belgian independence and Prince Leopold of Saxe Coburg was created Leopold I, King of the Belgians. The Treaty of London further saw that Belgium had freedom of both religion and press and an elected parliament controlled public finances. This was the famous 'Scrap of Paper' which the Kaiser tore up in 1914.

From the time of Leopold I, who became king in 1831, the Saxe Coburg line has ruled the country. Leopold II came to the throne in 1865 and was to bring the Congo under Belgian control. During the eighties there was as much glamour and glory attached to the exploration of unknown Africa as exists today in going to the moon. One of the most celebrated explorers of that time was Henry Morton Stanley who was put on the payroll of the king. Stanley became famous by getting the newspaper scoop of the century for the *New York Herald* when he found Livingstone in the forests of Africa. The hazardous journey ended with the oft-repeated phrase 'Doctor Livingstone, I presume' which were the words Stanley used when greeting the Scotsman in the steamy jungle. Later he was to find Emin Pasha, a German who had been made Governor of the Equatorial Province of the Sudan during the Gordon campaign. The Europeans who had opposed the Mahdi were either dead or slaves and it was feared that a similar fate had overtaken Emin Pasha.

Stanley returned with Emin after a three-year expedition. He was always drawn back to Africa and seemed to lead a charmed life there. He wrote of his various discoveries, the most fascinating of which was the Congo waterway which pierced through the very heart of Africa. He was immediately aware of commercial possibilities along the river and the one other man who grasped the same idea was Leopold II. The king approached Stanley in 1878 and in November of that year Stanley committed himself to the king's ideas. The explorer was to make a further expedition 'to prove that the Congo natives were susceptible of civilization and that the Congo basin was rich enough to repay exploitation' for a *'Comité d'études du Haut Congo'*.

Stanley set off for the Congo again and in the ensuing five years accomplished much that the king wanted. The *Comité* in the meantime changed its name to that of *'Association Internationale du Congo'* to obtain the recognition of America and Europe for its transformation into an independent state, under the sovereignty of King Leopold II. In 1908 the vast Congo was annexed to Belgium. On 30 June 1960 Belgium accorded full independence to her colony.

The Congo Museum at Temruren on the outskirts of Brussels is fascinating. The very atmosphere of Africa can be felt as soon as you step through the entrance. You will find an interesting assortment of strange items such as polished woods, carved ivories, gems, peculiar musical instruments, war canoes, stuffed animals and exotic fruit trees.

Albert I came to the throne in 1909 and was beloved and admired for his self-sacrificing but courageous role during the First World War after which he and Queen Elizabeth rode in triumph into Brussels at the head of the Allied troops. He was mounted on a snow-white horse and at his right side rode the future king of England George VI. Unfortunately King Albert fell to his death in 1934 during a climbing expedition near Namur. Leopold III married Princess Astrid of Sweden who was also killed in a tragic car accident. The King's brother ruled later as Regent until 1951 when Leopold's son, Baudouin, became King. Baudouin bears the same name as five crusader counts of Flanders who ruled in Jerusalem during the twelfth and thirteenth centuries. King Baudouin married Dona Fabiola di Mora y Aragon on 15 December 1960. The royal couple live in a palace in Laeken, a suburb about a mile and a half north of Brussel's North Station. The surrounding park is spacious and stately. Near the 230-foot high Japanese Tower, bought by Leopold II from the Paris Exposition of 1900, is the Royal Church of Laeken where members of the royal family are entombed.

The present two main parties in the Belgian parliament are not large enough to win elections outright with the result that there have been several coalitions of Catholics, Socialists and Liberals since the Second World War. The King plays an important role by making it his business to discover the most likely politician to make a good premier. If the man cannot form a coalition the King must find someone who can.

The British have always had an affinity for 'Little Belgium'. This was especially emphasized during the First World War when a tiny section of Belgium in the extreme north-west never fell to the Germans. The British Commonwealth retained a foothold at Ypres, known to the troops as 'Wipers', during the four-year siege and could not be moved. Countless cemeteries bear witness. The enemy began shelling this small town on 7 October 1914 and did not cease until 14 October 1918.

Among Englishmen who have become enamoured of Belgium are many well-known writers: Anthony Trollope says, 'And a nice little kingdom it is, full of old towns, fine Flemish pictures and interesting Gothic architecture'; Robert Louis Stevenson wrote of its charming canals and rivers, Thomas More discussed and wrote his *Utopia* there and had it printed at Louvain University in 1516.

Perhaps the link between the two countries has been further strengthened by a similar sense of humour. When M Paul Henri Spaak was Foreign Minister of the Belgian government-in-exile for four years in London during the Second World War, he was told that he looked like Winston Churchill himself and spoke like Charles Boyer. He replied quickly with a smile – 'I wish it were the other way round'.

2. Brussels and the Province of Brabant

Brussels, capital of the European Economic Community, capital of Belgium, capital of NATO and capital of the province of Brabant, is despite these grand-sounding titles a small city with a population of a mere one and a half million. Its parks and wide tree-lined avenues give a feeling of spaciousness despite the growing network of underpasses and ringroads. Because of its size one of the delights of Brussels is that a 10- or 15-minute drive can take you from the heart of the town into the countryside. Indeed, a 40-minute bus ride from the Place Rouppe will not only take you from the heart of the city through the charming Bois de la Cambre and the forest of Soignes but beyond Brussels to the rolling pastureland and memorial mound of Waterloo.

Brussels is full of surprises. Buildings range from fantasies such as Leopold II's Chinese pavilion and Japanese pagoda to the science fiction Atomium. This represents a molecule of iron magnified two billion times and, together with its nuclear museum, was created for the 1958 World's Fair.

Without doubt the crown of this Queen-among-cities is the Grand Place, probably the most beautiful square in Europe. Like Brussels itself it is not vast nor does it boast unique monuments but it has a captivating ambience not found elsewhere. It has been called theatrical and certainly its Baroque guildhouses with their scrolled façades, the Hotel de Ville and ornate Maison du Roi would make a splendid backdrop for a pageant. If you half-close your eyes you can imagine the spectacular jousting that

used to take place between the Dukes of Brabant and Burgundy
on the flagstones.

The greater part of the south side of the Grand Place is
occupied by the Hotel de Ville. One of the two wings was begun
half a century before the other so that the right side is shorter
than the left, which dates from 1410, and is richer in design.
The façade of this magnificent building is embellished with
statues and friezes. The decorative tracery work is almost as delicate as the tapestries now displayed within. This town hall is a
beautiful example of fifteenth-century Gothic architecture and
was completed in 1449 by Jan Van Ruysbroeck, architect to
Philip the Good. Its fine tower is square at the base but emerges
above the rooftop into an octagonal shape edged by four small
spires and topped by a 16-foot copper statue of Saint Michael,
patron saint of the city, wrought in 1454 by Martin van Rode.
This unique building still functions as a seat of municipal government and is open to visitors. During the summer, glamour is
added in the evenings by *Son et Lumière* displays. Flood lighting
throws into sharp relief the gargoyles which glare downward at
the palatial staircase, guarded by benign heraldic lions at either
end. The beasts hold upright shields in their front paws and
their manes are smoothed back from their foreheads as if thousands of passers-by had stroked them.

To gain entrance you must pass through the massive doorway
edged with statuary into a courtyard and from there take the
door to the right where guides wait to conduct tours. By Belgian
law bridal couples must have a civil marriage ceremony as well
as a church one so the Hotel de Ville is always booked up months
ahead for such occasions. A major domo in eighteenth-century
costume ushers couple after couple into the richly ornate Salle
de Mariage. Outside in the Grand Place local people and tourists
sit around the outdoor café tables sipping wine or coffee, watching with interest as the brides and grooms with their families
come and go.

Across the Grand Place from the Hotel de Ville is the smaller
but very ornate Maison du Roi which also houses municipal

offices and a museum. Although never a royal residence, its name derives from Charles v who had the building reconstructed at the beginning of the sixteenth century in a mixture of Gothic and early Renaissance styles. It is also known as the 'Bread House' for the original building on this site was a bread market. It was then turned into law courts and, ironically enough, later into a prison. It also once served as the tax and administrative centre for the Dukes of Burgundy. The Maison du Roi underwent several other transformations with different owners before its acquisition in 1860 by the city of Brussels. Its museum, as well as extensive porcelain and ceramic exhibits, has an exceptional collection of standard measures used by Brussels' merchants before the introduction of the metric system. Other treasures include Pieter Breughel's famous painting 'The Wedding Procession' and the extensive and international wardrobe of the little Manneken-Pis.

Brussels suffered terribly in 1695 from a bombardment by the French under Marshal Villeroi who blasted the city with red-hot shot. Four thousand houses and 16 churches were burnt down and much of the Grand Place was razed to the ground. Miraculously the Hotel de Ville escaped with little damage and less than four years later the Grand Place began to take shape once more.

As you walk around the square, where cars are forbidden to park during the day, you will be able to distinguish some of the fascinating guild houses by their signs and statues. Number 16 is the House of the Millers and has a windmill between the busts of two Brabant dukes. The House of the Tanners, number 15, is known as The Fortune and here a blindfolded woman is shown emptying a bag of coins. Number 19, La Bourse, has a purse as its sign. The House of Tailors, number 25, has a statue of Saint Boniface and a plaque by his side shows a pair of shears.

The Haberdashers' Guild, at number 7, has a statue of Saint Nicholas, who is their patron saint, and a charming golden fox over the doorway gives the building the name of The Fox. A sixteenth-century house, number 36, also rejoices in a similar name The Little Fox! A few famous restaurants lie behind some

of the gilded façades. The Brabant coat-of-arms is above the door
of the small, exclusive 'La Couronne' and number 9, which has
a swan with outspread wings above the entrance, is the well-
known restaurant 'The Swan'. At one time it was the House of
the Butchers.

On the roof of number 10, next to The Swan, there is an
equestrian statue of the eighteenth-century governor of the Low
Countries, Charles of Lorraine. He holds his right arm out in
greeting. This building, known as The Golden Tree, was the
Brewers House and appropriately enough is today a Brewery
Museum. These guild houses are unique ornaments in this elegant square and, to add to its beauty, there is a flower market
every morning. On Sunday mornings the centre of the square
dons a new guise and becomes, for some strange reason, a bird
market.

It is difficult, on a sunny, warm day with the flamboyant
buildings literally glittering with gold, to believe that the Grand
Place has witnessed many scenes of drama – executions, revolution and the departures of occupying armies. There were feuds
between rival guilds; Egmont, Hoorn and other gallant men were
put to death under the shadow of these ancient buildings. The
French Republic was proclaimed here by Dumouriez.

If you leave the square through the arches of 'The Star', the
house next to 'The Swan', you come to Everard 't Serclaes'
monument commemorating this fourteenth-century defender of
Brussels and you are suddenly conscious of a warring past. Serclaes died in this house and superstition has it that, if you rub
the arm of this fallen patriot or the nose of his faithful dog and
make a wish, it will come true. Both places are polished bright
by thousands of hands. The charming little dog, awake by his
dead master's side, is as enticing to touch as Aladdin's lamp or
Peter Pan's little animals in London's Kensington Gardens.

Above the statue of Serclaes there are three carved plaques
depicting scenes of his life and death. One shows him leading his
small force which saved Brussels from Louis de Male. The second
is of Wenceslas of Luxembourg and his wife Jeanne of Brabant

entering Brussels in triumph. The last scene is of the burning of the Castle of Gaasbeek which was carried out in revenge for Serclaes' death. A woman plucking a chicken is sometimes pointed out in the right-hand corner of the last plaque. She is a symbol of the Battle of Bastweiler in 1371, when defeat came about because people paid more attention to eating than to making munitions.

To the left of this statue there is a joint memorial to Charles Buls who was renowned for saving many historic buildings and to the architects of the Grand Place. The street leading away from the square is also called after Charles Buls and, if you continue walking along this for a few minutes, it becomes the Rue de l'Etuve. When you reach the corner of Rue du Chene on the left side there is the statue of the famous or infamous Manneken-Pis. He is a cherubic little figure, a mere 24 inches tall, and few people leave Brussels without seeing him. He is urinating into a marble basin, his right arm crooked on his hip and an angelic expression on his face. He never fails to draw smiles from passers-by, while tourists endlessly take photographs of him.

The whimsical, tiny Manneken-Pis dates from 1619 but the statue was destroyed by a vandal and was not recast until 1817. It is not known what inspired the sculptor Duquesnoy to fashion the figure although stories are many. One states that he was a nobleman's son and got lost in a forest. When he was found it was in the same position as he can be seen today and his father was so overjoyed to find him that he had the statue made. Another legend says that a wicked fairy discovered him thus and cast a spell that assured people would always see him just as she had the first time. He personifies Brussels ribaldry in a charming way. The statue was stolen several times and when French soldiers were caught making off with it Louis xv returned it clothed in a gold-embroidered suit, a copy of the robes of a French marquis. This started a spate of gifts of clothing from international sources which would make any little boy envious. His 250 suits include all kinds of uniforms and national costumes as well as sports outfits such as that of a Canadian hockey player.

On special occasions the statuette is decked out in one of these but at other times, even on the coldest winter day, the Manneken-Pis remains his naked happy self.

From the Manneken-Pis take the Rue du Chene and number 27 on the right is the Schott Museum which has some interesting fifteenth- and sixteenth-century wood carvings. Around to the right beyond the museum there is a section of the old town wall. Extensive reconstruction work is being carried out in the area but if you go across the Place de Dinant and to the Rue de l'Empereur, you will see a section of twelfth-century fortification on the far side of the road which has a medieval tower. This is known as 'Anneesen's Tower' and here the gentleman of that name, dean of the guildsmen, was imprisoned because of his opposition in 1719 to the reigning Austrian government. Later he was beheaded in the Grand Place.

Near the Grand Place off the Rue Marche aux Herbes you will come upon the 700-foot long glass-domed Galeries Saint Hubert. There are several covered galleries in Brussels with gift shops, cafés and boutiques which come into their own particularly on rainy days. The Galeries Saint Hubert is the best known and was the first shopping arcade of this type to be built in Europe. It was opened in 1846 and its long shop windows are flanked by flat brown and white marble columns and walls, which would cost an astronomical sum today. Above the fan lights the flags of the Common Market add colour, regarded steadfastly by life-size marble statues in niches. When the sun shines it casts checkerboard patterns from the glass roofing on the flagged footway, windows glistening with the brilliance of gems, and picks out the delicacy of the handmade lace, succulent chocolates or fashion creations. Whatever the weather, from the cafés comes the delicious aroma of freshly ground coffee.

Crossing the Galeries Saint Hubert almost in the centre between the Galerie du Roi and the Galerie de la Reine, is the engaging Rue des Bouchers, a narrow sloping street of little restaurants, each with its own specialities, where you can obtain a meal typical of practically any country you wish to name. These little cafés are not pretentious but the food is served with panache. The last time I had a meal there I had just returned from Tunisia and chose number 39, 'Chez Karim', to have lunch I ordered 'brik', egg folded in paper-thin pastry and deep fried so that the whole is crispy but the yolk soft, and then cous cous. The meal was as delicious as the one served in just such a café in Tunis itself. Off to the left of this street there is an even narrower one called Rue des Petite Bouchers with more eating places and a marionette theatre.

There are innumerable other small restaurants and cafés around the Grand Place and the streets surrounding it, for the Belgians, like the French, take eating extremely seriously and like plenty of choice. Menus are chalked up outside or can be read behind glass plaques, thus you know your commitment before entering. There is something to suit all tastes and pockets.

An alternative way of leaving the Grand Place is by the Rue de la Colline leading out of the north-east corner. Passing the enticing window of Godiva's hand-made chocolates on the left, if you can, you come to another shopping arcade. Beyond this a few seconds' walk brings you to the Bourse, the stock exchange building, and on the left the partially hidden Saint Nicholas' Church. Beside its porch is one of the most charming statues in Brussels – the little milkmaid by Marc Devos. She is holding a pitcher, pouring milk into a bowl and is strangely reminiscent of Vermeer's famous 'Kitchen Maid', a portrait of just such another sturdy country lass also pouring milk into a bowl. The milkmaid is backed by a lattice work of leaves during the summer which gives her a suitable backdrop.

Inside Saint Nicholas's Church to your right there is a plaque which gives an outline of its history and reads :

The origin of this Church is closely connected with the coming into existence of the city of Brussels, in the eleventh and twelfth centuries. It was originally intended to be a market church dedicated to Saint Nicholas, one of the merchants' favourite saints. Originally of Romanesque architecture and style it was later enlarged and transformed into Gothic style. The choir dates from about AD 1381. During the religious troubles of the sixteenth century it was sacked and destroyed as was the fate of the Grand Place in the immediate vicinity during the bombardment of AD 1625. In AD 1740 the collapse of the tower further contributed to its ruin. However, after each of these unfortunate events the church was restored. The present façade dates from AD 1956.

A gallery high above the nave is floodlit through pillars and a painting 'Mary with the sleeping Child', about two feet square and reputed to be a Rubens, hangs on a column in the left aisle. Mary is shown in a red robe praying over an infant Christ in bed whose sleeping features face the onlooker. About 12 feet above this portrait you can see a black cannon ball embedded in the column with the date 1695 marked beneath it, a reminder of fighting with the French at that time.

Close to Saint Nicholas' Church is one of my favourite restaurants, 'Au Vieux Temps', which has a sign above the passage leading to it off the Marche aux Herbes. It is in the middle price bracket and has an old-time atmosphere and it is advisable to book a table for it is well known and not very large.

From the Marche aux Herbes you can catch a glimpse of the Cathedral of Saint Michael and, to the right of this towering building, there is a modern square with Brussels Central Station, the Belgian Tourist Office and the large Sabena Air Terminal. You can arrive here directly by train from the Airport. Sabena has some 68 flights a week from Heathrow to Brussels in co-operation with British Airways and also regular flights from Gatwick to Ostend in collaboration with Dan Air giving easy access to the Belgian coast. Sabena are also in the transatlantic big league with two jumbo flights a day to New York.

The majestic cathedral of Saint Michael is built on a steep slope and is entered by a side door. It is Gothic in style and its famed stained-glass windows, some 70 feet in height, were given by Charles v and other members of the royal family. These were made from drawings by Bernard Van Orley. Charles of Lorraine and many Dukes of Brabant are buried to the left of the chancel. The seventeenth-century pulpit is flanked by semi-spiral staircases with a carved eagle on the banister on one side and a peacock on the other. The pulpit itself, carved from a single tree trunk, has lifesize figures of Adam and Eve leaving the Garden of Eden, strangely enough fully clothed. Eve with long flowing hair still clasps an apple in her hand.

In what is often called the 'upper' town of Brussels there are two delightful squares cheek-by-jowl known as the Grand Sablon and the Petit Sablon divided by the Rue de la Regence which runs from the Palais de Justice to the Place Royal. The Palais de Justice is Brussel's Law Courts, said to be the most enormous building of its kind in Europe. Certainly it is on a most commanding site and overlooks most of the rest of the city. Viewing telescopes are placed at various points to one side of the building and, if you insert a coin, you can also hear a tape recording which will describe the various districts and buildings you can see. Making up in size what it lacks in beauty, it has 245 rooms besides 27 court and committee chambers, a floor area of 280,000 square feet and from the ground floor to the top of its dome the building is 385 feet high. Larger than Saint Peter's in Rome, this sprawling edifice needs 15 tons of coal a day to heat it.

Spread out directly below the plateau of the Palais de Justice lies the Montmartre of Brussels, the beloved quarter known as Les Marolles. It is criss-crossed with shopping streets and alleyways. Pieter Breughel the Elder was born here and, once you have strolled through this populous quarter with its neon signs, colourful characters and spicy smells, you will no longer be puzzled to know why his two sons, Pieter and Jan, were known as 'Hell' and 'Velvet'. 'Hell' was also known as 'Infernal' for his paintings were of conflagrations, sieges, witches and devils. His younger brother 'Velvet' painted miniatures, flowers and landscapes. The Breughel Museum is at 132 Rue Haute, the house where Breughel the Elder lived for the last six years of his life.

3 *Harvesting witloof*

4 *Sampling snails at a stall in the Brussels antique market*

5 *Cat signpost at Ypres*

6 *Guild houses on the quayside in Ghent*

His tomb is in the nearby Eglise de la Chapelle which dates back to the twelfth century. The Infanta Isabella presented a charming Spanish statue of the Virgin Mary by Becerra to this church. It is known as 'Our Lady of Solitude' and the head is draped with a black lace mantilla.

Every morning from 9 a.m. to 1 p.m. there is a sort of 'Petticoat Lane' market in the Place du Jeu de Balle in Les Marolles known as the 'Flea Market'. You can buy anything and everything, old (and new!) antiques, books, prints, china, jewellery, clothes and, now and then among all the dross, something special you may treasure. But no matter if you buy or not there is a carnival atmosphere here that you will find difficult to resist.

The square of the Petit Sablon is attractive and unusual in that it is a small park surrounded by wrought ironwork decorated with 48 bronze figures in medieval costume representing sixteenth-century trade guilds. It is interesting to conjecture what guild each statue signifies. A clockmaker holds a clock and keys, a boatman a paddle, a baker has a bread basket on his head full of loaves, an artist a palette, wine merchant a goblet and a furniture craftsman holds a little chair.

You can stroll inside the little park or rest on one of the benches. There is a fountain and also statues of prominent people of the sixteenth and seventeenth centuries. Here you will quickly recognize the bearded Gerard Mercator, the famous Antwerp geographer, holding his globe, and the other map-maker Oretelius. There is a fine statue of William the Silent and, at the far end of the garden, figures of Count Egmont and Count Hoorn, the latter with his hand resting on Egmont's shoulder.

Immediately behind this little park is the Palais d'Egmont which now houses various public bodies. Should you stroll through the palace gardens you will come upon a replica of Frampton's famous Peter Pan statue opposite a children's playground. The original is in London's Kensington Gardens. It was presented to the children of Brussels by the children of London. If you walk through the nearby gate you will find yourself in sharp contrast close to the entrance of the Hilton Hotel.

Wedged between the Petit and the Grand Sablon there is the Church of Notre Dame de Sablon or, to give it its correct name, Notre Dame des Victoires. It has grown into Gothic splendour from a small chapel built by crossbowmen in 1304. It is one of Brussels most beautiful churches with a lovely rose window in the south-east transept and eleven 46-foot high stained-glass windows. On 3 November each year a mass to Saint Hubert, patron saint of huntsmen, is held. If you go through the door facing the Petit Sablon there is a statue of Saint Hubert just inside the entrance. The saint's right hand is raised in blessing and he holds a Bible in his left hand. A stag lies at rest by his right side sheltered by his cloak. Between the stag's antlers there is a cross with a hanging Christ.

On Saturdays and Sunday mornings in the Grand Sablon there is an antique market where both local people and tourists throng. Among the bric-a-brac there are undoubtedly treasures of one kind or another – old maps, books, engravings, silver, pewter, crystal, furniture and jewellery. If you are hungry there are stalls selling snails and other delicacies giving off tempting aromas. Even if there is a drizzle the market makes a gay scene for the stalls are protected with green and red striped awnings and umbrellas, the various lanes between them marked out by little tubs of bay trees. In the centre of the melée stands the serene Minerva fountain presented to Brussels long ago by the Count of Allesbury, Count Bruce. This was in gratitude for Belgian hospitality during his exile from England on religious grounds. The antique shops surrounding the square itself are also intriguing and there are nearly as many people on the pavement as in the central market so that it is almost impossible to park your car. Patisseries with delicious bread, buns and cakes are open on Sunday morning for a short time to expand your waistline while you ponder on your next bargain.

A stone's throw from the Grand Sablon there is the dignified Place Royale designed by Barnaby Guimard in the eighteenth century at the request of Charles of Lorraine. The equestrian statue of Godefroy de Bouillon is in the centre. He was born at

Baisy in Brabant, led the First Crusade, was asked to be the first king of Jerusalem, which he refused, and eventually died in Palestine. King Leopold I ordered the statue in 1843. It shows the Count holding his standard aloft before setting forth on the First Crusade in 1099.

In the left-hand corner of the Place Royale was 'Old England', a favourite shop in Brussels with a tearoom on the first floor where you could get an excellent view over the capital. Unhappily it has now moved.

The Palais des Beaux Arts, Brussels most famous museum, stretches along the Rue de Regence from the Place Royale. It covers a great expanse of ground and has sculptures as well as galleries of priceless paintings. The grandiose building also includes the Royal Library, the Museum of Modern Art, concert and lecture halls – the last two having entrances from the Rue Ravenstein or, by descending an open stairway, from the Rue de la Regence. It would take several days to examine the masterpieces in this vast palace designed by the architect Victor Horta, an exponent of the Art Nouveau style of architecture in his day. The museum has such a huge collection, some 45,000 works, that much of it cannot be on display.

The great Flemish painters are all here. World-renowned names like Rubens, David Teniers, Bosch, Jordaens, Memling, Metsys, Breughel and many more. Each person will have his own favourite among the masterpieces. In a section by itself and so fragile that it can only be lit dimly is 'The Adoration of the Maji', reputed to be by Breughel the Elder, although not in his usual style. Its method of display is similar to da Vinci's cartoon in London's National Gallery.

There are two remarkable things about the Lucas Cranach painting 'Venus and Love'. Like the Veni de Milo and de Medici she is nude but wears a becoming hat, a necklace and a transparent stole. Moreover the story about the painting before it arrived in the museum in 1938 shows an extraordinary coincidence.

The Baron Cassel had had the top part of the painting in his private collection for some years. On a visit abroad he could not believe his eyes when he saw what he was certain were the legs of his Venus in the window of an antique shop. What was an even greater surprise was that the signature was that of Lucas Cranach. On the right side of the legs was the naked winged figure of a rather puzzled cupid, his left chubby hand held to his forehead like Rodin's The Thinker. The Baron bought the painting and on his return home was more than delighted to find that it did indeed fit the bottom of his canvas and that the slender legs belonged to his Venus. The goddess's right hand was placed protectively over cupid and her smile is as mysterious as that of the Mona Lisa. Cupid is said to have been born to Venus late in life and the ancestry of Eros, as he is also called, is not very clear in mythology. However, artists have always made much of this wanton imp and the arrows he shoots in careless mischief, some tipped with gold to quicken and some with lead to deaden the pulse of love.

Baron Cassel invited Doctor Leo van Puyvelde, head curator of the Museum of Fine Arts, to dine with him one night in 1938. During the evening the Baron said that after his death some of his paintings would be bequeathed to the museum including Cranach's 'Venus and Love'. When the time came to leave, the curator said that he could never again accept an invitation to the Baron's house. 'Why?' asked the Baron in surprise. 'Because,' replied the curator simply, 'I might say I wish you were dead knowing that only then could we have such a charming painting as Venus and Love'. Both men laughed and there and then took the portrait in a cab to the museum.

In room five, four paintings stand out in my mind, one being Frans Hals portrait of Johannes Hoornbeek. The sitter appears to be listening to the onlooker and patiently awaits his turn to give an opinion, perhaps on something religious, as he holds a Bible in his left hand. He is a middle-aged man, content with his life, wearing a well-cut suit fitting snugly over his stomach and a spotless broad white collar, tailored perfectly yet not pinching his rather protruding neckline. Then there is the portrait, also by

Hals, of three happy children the very essence of joyous youth. There is Rembrandt's painting of Van Barnbeeck with black hat donned at a jaunty angle and his snow-white collar edged with impeccable lace. The realistic death pallor of the dead woman's face in 'The Dead' makes you look away momentarily but then you turn again to admire her peaceful expression.

Da Vinci's 'Leda and the Swan' is in another gallery and is amusing and usually brings a smile to onlookers' faces. Leda with a mysteriously happy countenance snuggles up closely to her sleek swan in a rustic setting while cherubic rosy children have broken out of eggs at their feet, one emerging buttocks first.

Between October and the end of May midday concerts take place in the Rubens Room on Wednesdays. If hungry you can have a sandwich snack beforehand.

Also in the Place Royale is the former palace of King Leopold III and Queen Astrid. Close by is the last remaining sixteenth-century palace of the Burgundian Court now converted into the Hotel Ravenstein where many ceremonial dinners and receptions are held. Anne of Cleves, fourth of King Henry VIII's six wives, was born in this palace.

The King's palace faces a large formal park designed by André Le Notre, the seventeenth-century French landscape architect, who laid out the gardens of Versailles, Saint Cloud and Fontainebleau. The palace has been rebuilt over the site of former royal residences and today King Baudouin and Queen Fabiola spend most of their time in the less formal palace at Laeken.

The park is flanked on the opposite side by the Palais de la Nation, the Parliament buildings whose classical façade was designed by Guimard in 1783.

Beyond these buildings along the Rue Royale you come to the Colonne du Congres. This high column with a statue of Leopold I on the summit is reminiscent of Nelson's column in Trafalgar Square – complete with pigeons! From the top, after a climb of nearly 200 steps, there is a wonderful view. On either side of an ever-burning flame at the base there is a tomb. These are the resting places of two of Belgium's unknown soldiers who died in the First World War and the Second World War. The four statues surrounding the column represent the four freedoms of worship, education, association and the press for this monument, designed by Joseph Poelaert, also commemorates the first National Assembly of independent Belgium in 1831.

The main shopping areas of Brussels are described usually as 'downtown' or 'uptown'. 'Uptown' includes the Rue Royale and the fashionable Avenue Louise which debouches to one side of the Palais de Justice. This has a series of ultra-modern covered galleries with elegant shops, boutiques and café terraces. One called the 'Garden of Louise' near the top of the avenue is only half-covered in with an outdoor café surrounded with flower beds and a fountain. If it is too sunny or humid there is always 'Watney's Louise Pub' for lunch or a cool beer. This is closed on Sundays and public holidays. When it is raining there is no need to hurry by 'Feraud's' or 'Butch's' large windows full of trendy clothes and exclusive men's wear.

Windows in the Avenue Louise itself tempt shoppers with exquisite jewellery, bone china, couture clothes and mouth-watering displays of chocolate. Belgium has a well-deserved reputation for hand-made chocolates and a chain of shops known as 'Godiva' have fresh ones daily. Even if you just choose an ounce or two they are carefully arranged in tiny boxes and wrapped as if you had bought a pound or more. Hand-made leather goods are beautifully finished. Handbags and wallets are good buys and often less expensive than in Britain. 'Dujardin' is the best children's store. Val Saint Lambert crystal, traditional in design, is worth considering. As you go further along the dignified Avenue Louise, shops, hotels and restaurants give way to villas. These are interspersed with characteristic, turn-of-the-century houses whose front doors not only have charming fanlights above the lintels but short flights of steps leading up from the pavement. The latter are usually flanked by wrought iron banisters.

In these houses, where the kitchen windows are usually half below ground level, the kitchens themselves are still referred to affectionately as 'caves'.

In the 'downtown' shopping area the most important boulevard is the Adolphe Max named after a Burgomaster of Brussels who became a national hero during the First World War. He defied the Germans in every possible way, the result being that they threw him in prison for four years.

The Boulevard Adolphe Max is particularly attractive because of its ornamental wrought iron work, especially the small balconies. A familiar note is struck by the W H Smith English bookshop at number 71-75, complete with English tea room on the first floor. Another attraction is the Metropole shopping arcade veering off to the west side of the avenue. The light from the domed glass skylight picks out the 'acropolis like' ladies who valiantly support the second floor on their heads in true Grecian style. The Adolphe Max then debouches into the Place de Brouckere, the Piccadilly Circus of the Belgian capital, and becomes Boulevard Anspach.

The north end of Adolphe Max joins the Place Rogier where the first part of the vast Manhattan Centre project is now complete. To date it comprises the Sheraton and Lendi hotels, two floors of shopping arcades, a 30-storey office block with conference and exhibition halls and beneath it all parking for 1,000 cars. It is only about five minutes' walk from the World Trade Centre and the North Railway Station which has a direct rail link to Brussels airport.

The lobby of the 31-storey Sheraton Hotel connects with the shopping centre. It has one of the highest swimming pools in the world on the roof with a sundeck and is the largest hotel in Brussels. Its 476 rooms each have a colour television, a five-channel radio-music system, air conditioning and a mini bar. The American Coffee Shop is open for all meals. An intimate restaurant, 'Les Comtes de Flandre', serves delicious food and there is also a gastronomic roof-top restaurant. Perhaps the most unusual thing about the Sheraton is that it is the first building in Europe with an exterior lift attached to its façade. It is made of anodised aluminium with heated 'Raybel' glass through which visitors have a widening panorama of the city as they are whisked up into the air.

The Lendi Hotel is also part of Manhattan Centre. Owned by the Swiss chain of hotels of the same name, its three restaurants are designed on an open space plan interconnected by a spiral ramp instead of stairs. This gives a feeling of intimacy and at the same time spaciousness. The Lendi is also unusual in that two-thirds of its rooms are singles.

Hotels have personalities of their own; they charm, fascinate or annoy according to the whims and outlook of their guests. For instance on the opposite side of Place Rogier stands the older Palace Hotel whose foyer has echoed the footsteps of many famous people.

An example of the foibles which such places cater for dates back to the years between the wars when the late Aga Khan was a frequent visitor at the Palace. It was always arranged that the porters who handled his luggage were shorter in stature than His Excellency as he preferred it that way.

Another anecdote attributed to the Palace is more unusual. A party of foreigners had assembled in the foyer on an extremely hot day to await their courier for a sightseeing tour. One man suddenly started to undress, neatly folding his clothes as he removed them. As members of the staff approached to remonstrate, he completed the removal of his underclothes and then quickly began to dress again, explaining that it was far too hot for him to wear his vest and underpants. These he handed to the astonished hall porter.

When I visited Bouillon I had a long talk with Raymond Bonvin, the owner of the Hotel de la Poste, who had been manager of the Palace during the last war and he told me an amusing story about Churchill. It appears that Sir Winston lunched with the Prince Regent at the Palace shortly after the war was over. The luncheon was a great success, both participants enjoyed their food and wine and remained sometime after the meal was over, talking together. They were the last two guests to leave the dining room and went to retrieve their hats. The hat-check girl was so excited about the two famous gentlemen visiting the hotel that she could not remember which of the two remaining hats belonged to Sir Winston as the Prince gestured his guest forward. One hat was brand new, the other very old. The girl made a quick choice and presented the old hat to Sir Winston, the older man, and the new one to the younger Prince. The two men smiled their thanks and holding the hats went to the foyer to await a car. As they left the hotel Sir Winston started to light a cigar while the Prince donned the hat he was holding. It came down over his ears. 'Your Majesty, you have purloined my new hat', cried Churchill laughing and passed the old hat to the Prince. Both men put on their rightful headgear and, still laughing merrily, stepped into the waiting limousine.

Contemporary Brussels has many new hotels rubbing shoulders with the famous old ones like the Plaza, Palace and Amigo. The latter tucked away behind the Grand Place on a corner near Everard 't Serclaes' monument, has a foyer which boasts the same flagstones as the pavement outside. Many of its rooms and suites are in Empire and Directoire style.

Of the new hotels the glass towers of the Hilton and Westbury challenge the ever rising office blocks. The Royal Windsor is within easy walking distance of the Central Station and Sabena Air terminal. Its Royal Chophouse is on the mezzanine floor in a Victorian setting and it has an English-style pub, the Duke of Wellington, with the same type of décor on the ground floor where you can have snacks and beer. A Holiday Inn opened near Brussels Airport in 1971 and there are others in Bruges, Liège and Tournai. Grand Metropolitan's Europa Hotel with 250 rooms rises at the end of the long Rue de la Loi near the EEC building where the flags of the Common Market Countries fly outside the cruciform headquarters adding splashes of colour against the sky. The EEC building draws people like a magnet as it promises much for the future. It is 13 storeys high with over 1,000 offices and is joined to the centre of town by two parallel

one-way boulevards. Its austere appearance is softened by surrounding flower beds and fountains.

From the European Common Market building you can see a
gigantic three-fold triumphal arch. On top there is a great Roman
chariot drawn by four bronze galloping horses and driven by a
figure representing Belgium. It symbolizes the progress of the
little kingdom during more than half a century of national independence. The great archway, erected by Leopold II in 1905, is
flanked by the Royal Museum of Art and History on one side
and by the Royal Museum of the Army on the other. The huge
buildings and archway together make up the famous Palais du
Cinquantenaire and act as the entrance to a park of the same
name laid out to celebrate the 50th anniversary of the founding
of Belgium.

If you walk or motor down the short Avenue J F Kennedy,
which leads from Place Schuman to the arch, you get an idea
of the layout of both the park and museums. The latter are full
of interesting items but take several hours to view properly. The
Art and History Museum is one of the best of its kind in Europe
and has collections of Egyptian, Greek and Asian antiquities not
to mention tapestries, carvings and porcelain. The Military
Museum runs the gamut from the Napoleonic wars up to the
Second World War.

Beyond the arch the Avenue de Tervuren, one of the finest
boulevards on the Continent, runs through the park. During its
length of seven miles it passes the Park of Woluwe, on through
the Forest of Soignes ending at the entrance to Tervuren Park
which was once a royal hunting reserve and covers some 500
acres. Here you can visit the Royal Central African Museum
commissioned by Leopold II. It was designed by the French
architect Charles Girault and is a smaller edition of plans he
made for the Petit Palais on the Champs Elysees in Paris. There
is an excellent zoology section and, if you enjoy the mask and
sculpture portion, you can buy copies of some of the works at
the entrance. The park itself is charming with terraced gardens
and places to stroll. There is also a restaurant, a lake where you

can hire boats in the summer and, close to the water, a small chapel dedicated to Saint Hubert which is said to be built over the spot where the saint died in 1617.

The Forest of Soignes, with its fine copper beeches, stretches out towards Waterloo but before leaving the Brussels area we must make one more call on the other side of the city. There is a lovely patrician house of the Gothic period in the suburb of Anderlecht which is well worth a visit for it was here that Erasmus the famous scholar, critic and wit lived in 1521.

Though born the illegitimate son of an obscure priest, Erasmus was courted throughout his life by Popes, Kings and Princes and his correspondents included all the great names of his day, among them Rabelais, Holbein, Durer, von Hutten and Sir Thomas More. Sometimes referred to as the 'Voltaire of the Renaissance', he detested anything that savoured of fanaticism or extremes. At a time when few people travelled, he did so widely and no matter where he was he wrote constantly. His great desire was to erase the superstitious deposit of centuries and disclose a simplified, rational Christianity in which all Europe could be united.

Erasmus, like most great men, had irrational likes and dislikes. Although he crossed the Channel to England several times he hated the sea – indeed he hated fish, claiming that 'his heart was Catholic but his stomach was Lutheran'. He found that white wine and beer disagreed with him, but like so many other people before and after him, could thoroughly enjoy the wines of Burgundy! Sayings of his are still used by us today: 'Call a spade a spade', 'One swallow does not make a summer', 'As plain as the nose on your face' and others.

Erasmus was born in Rotterdam and his statue there shows him clad in fifteenth-century robes and his famous black hat, his attention held by an open book in one hand with the other poised to turn a page. Legend has it that when the nearby steeple clock strikes the hour he does so!

Erasmus' house in Anderlecht is spacious in itself and has a delightful garden. At one time it was owned by a religious order but, because the famous humanist lived there, albeit for a short time, it is always known as 'Erasmus' House'. Strangely enough my husband and I visited it on Christmas Day, never dreaming that it would be open, but hoping to catch a glimpse of the garden, see the nearby Beguinage and perhaps go for a walk before returning to our hotel. It was only a 15-minute drive from the centre of Brussels and the house was easy to find because there were signs to it all the way. A red brick wall surrounds the garden and we walked through the gateway, skirted a small lawn surrounded by a tiny box hedge and found ourselves at the front door which was ajar. The curator was amused at our delight in finding the house open and gestured us in. We were completely alone, perhaps because no one had thought of visiting such a place on Christmas Day. The house was centrally heated and so well lit that the polished parquet floors gleamed. There was a pleasant smell of beeswax and it felt as if Erasmus himself might descend the central staircase at any moment.

The main salon called the 'Renaissance Room' has walls covered in blue and gold tooled leather. The most appealing room is the small library upstairs with its well-used polished table and brass-studded brown leather chairs. Many shelves of books include *In Praise of Folly* in several languages and some first editions. Coloured prints show Erasmus on some of his many journeys to Paris, Venice, Anderlecht, Basle and Gouda. A particularly fascinating one is of him having an animated discussion with Sir Thomas More, possibly about the latter's *Utopia.*

In the downstairs study there is a bronze bust of Erasmus on a plinth. For some inexplicable reason there is a round stained-glass miniature set in one of the diamond-paned windows of a man being disembowelled, which is far more horrifying than the skull on Erasmus' desk. Fortunately, being small it often goes unnoticed, but you cannot help wondering where it came from and how long it has been there.

The study has many portraits of Erasmus including one over the mantel-piece by Holbein. His gentle eyes follow you while you tread silently around the room until you halt by a clothes stand. You catch your breath for there hangs an old black hat like the ones you have seen in his pictures countless times. You would not be astonished if he walked in, took it off the wooden hook, winked knowingly and left.

Erasmus' House is closed on Tuesdays and Wednesdays and the rest of the week is open from ten o'clock to noon and from two until five in the afternoons.

You can return to the handsomely wooded Avenue de Tervuren if you wish to drive along the tourist route to Leuven (*French Louvain*) some 15 miles distant from Brussels. If you are in a hurry there is an autoroute which only takes a quarter of an hour.

Leuven, sometimes referred to as the most 'Martyred Town' in Belgium because of its terrible devastation during the last two World Wars, by some miracle has retained the shell of its superb Town Hall. It has such a wealth of elegant Gothic finials and ornamentation that you are left as speechless as when seeing Milan's Cathedral with its thousand spires for the first time. Having survived the bombing during the wars it is still not clear how the fragile decoration withstands inclement weather – but it does. It is considered one of the finest buildings of its kind in Belgium and continues to delight not only visitors but the many international students who attend Leuven's famous university.

Some of the buildings stem from the fourteenth, fifteenth and sixteenth centuries and many more were added around the town after 1918 when there was a lack of sites in Leuven itself. The university has had a unique record of scholarship for over five centuries. Erasmus inveighed here against bigotry and Justus Lipsius the German theologian, rector of Saint Thomas' at Leipzig and an expert on the history of early Christianity from a liberal point of view, also lectured here. It was on the presses of the university that Sir Thomas More's *Utopia* was first printed under the title *Libelius Vere Aureus*.

The university library, famous throughout Europe, was destroyed in the First World War when German troops laid the whole town waste during eight days of burning and looting. It was rebuilt under the direction of the American architect

Whitney Warren in neo-renaissance style. Its tower soared 285 feet and had a carillon of eight octaves. But as so often history repeated itself and the building was burnt down again on 10-11 May 1944. Once again, like a phoenix from its ashes, the library rose with generous funds, mostly from America. Its façade is decorated with a Belgian lion and an American eagle. Forty-eight stars, symbolic of the 48 states of America, embellish its new, high clock tower. Its spacious lecture hall is once again lined with books and a splendid collection of Spoelbergh de Lovenjoul porcelain.

The storms Leuven University has withstood are not only those of war. Latin was used for lectures at the beginning but during the nineteenth century this was replaced by French. As the university is in the Flemish area lectures in Flemish were given equal rights as from 1932. Language troubles were not helped by a steady flow of French-speaking students from the outside Catholic world wishing to attend the university. There were sporadic riots between the two language factions and this has resulted in the creation, in effect, of a new French-speaking university at Ottignies – now known as Louvain le Neuve – 12 miles away. The transfer is expected to take 10 years to complete and some facilities will continue to be shared. One feature which perhaps may not be is that the nearby beguinage in Leuven, one of the largest in the country, is now used for accommodation for married students. It is being restored and modernised but in appropriate style for this purpose.

The Collegiate Church of Saint Peter is across the main square from the Town Hall. Dating from the fifteenth century, it also suffered badly during both World Wars. It too has been rebuilt and retains a few original treasures. A painting by Dierick Bouts 'The Martyrdom of Saint Erasmus' was stolen by the Germans during each of the two World Wars and returned afterwards. A prized Madonna which vanished during the last war was recovered undamaged months later in some rubble. The Infant Christ sits on her knee and in her right hand she holds the emblem of Leuven University aloft.

The most outstanding treasure in the cathedral is another painting by Bouts of 'The Last Supper' which can be floodlit if you drop a coin in a box which operates a light switch. A most unusual feature is that through one of the windows you catch a glimpse of Leuven as the artist saw it when he did the painting. I found that the most appealing item was a fragile Gothic Sacramental Tower at the back of the church designed by the architect of the Town Hall.

Few visitors leave Brussels without a trip to Waterloo. It is a mere 45 minutes away if you catch the bus which leaves from the Place Rouppe in the centre of the city. This will decant you at the Lion Mound, an artificial pyramidal hill that rises up some 150 feet above the battle site. It is coated with green grass and shrubs and topped by a bronze lion cast from captured cannon. It was erected by the Belgians in honour of the Prince of Orange who was wounded during the fighting. You may climb the Lion Mound by 228 steps and thus get a view over the battlefield.

Even after a century and a half Waterloo remains a major tourist attraction. Those who know nothing about the battle understand the phrase – 'he met his Waterloo'. Byron's verse from *Childe Harold's Pilgrimage*, where he describes the Duchess of Richmond's ball the night before the battle took place, begins :

> *There was a sound of revelry by night*
> *And Belgium's capital had gathered then*
> *Her beauty and her Chivalry*

and is still quoted by schoolboys.

The battle, which caused Napoleon to lose all hope of recovering his empire, commenced just before noon on a Sunday morning in June 1815 and was over by nine o'clock that same night. The carnage was frightful for during those few hours 40,000 men and 10,000 horses were killed or wounded on a battlefield only two miles long and two-thirds of a mile across.

The results of that day in June were far reaching. Victory was to make Wellington the most influential personality in Europe. Victor Hugo described the battlefield as 'the corner of the earth that might have given Napoleon the world' had he won that day. Not only was he forced to flee but, on his return to Paris, was made to abdicate and, finding escape impossible, he surrendered to the British on 14 July – 'the most powerful, the most unwavering and the most generous of his foes'.

The controversial battle of Waterloo is still a subject for historians and several books have been written about it. For those interested in the actual battle there is the Wellington Museum where each phase of the day's operations can be followed with diagrams, maps and models. At the base of the Lion Mound there is also a building called 'Waterloo Panorama'. Inside you are surrounded by a great painting of the battle. You can easily spot Napoleon on his white mare named after Desirée, one of his early loves, and the Iron Duke on his gallant little chestnut Copenhagen.

Although both the great leaders were the same age, 46 years old, they differed in every other respect, even to the way in which they wore their cocked hats. Napoleon wore his in 'east/ west' fashion while Wellington preferred the conventional 'north/south' arrangement. Napoleon carried too much weight and was not in good health, the Duke slender and at the peak of his form. Napoleon wished to conquer the world with men who thought him invincible; Wellington treated fighting as a profession and at Waterloo led what he called an 'infamous army'. The Duke was austere and Napoleon luxury loving. It is said that, when the latter fled and his coach was captured, two million pounds worth of diamonds were discovered in the lining of his spare uniform. His toilet articles were of gold and a silver chamber pot is a trophy of one of the cavalry regiments of the British Army to this day.

In the 'Waterloo Panorama' you can identify the famous farms which served as strong points such as Hougoumont, La Haie Sainte and Belle Alliance but it is far more rewarding to go and see them in reality. A grass track leads to Hougoumont chapel and farmhouse. No turnstiles or soft drink stands spoil the atmosphere for Hougoumont is still a farm today and the

7 Small boy attired for the Binche carnival

understanding owner does not object to visitors. Hens scratch for worms outside the famous little chapel and the barns opposite are full of pedigree cows. Hougoumont was the hinge for the Allied line and was held by a battalion of English guards. Against it whole divisions of French cavalry were hurled continuously. When they finally forced their way into the farmyard it was to meet a murderous fire from every window, casement and wall. The damaged chapel with its tiny bell tower is much as it was when men fought for it. You enter through a weather-beaten door, the bars of whose grille have been reinforced. Inside, the brick floor is uneven. On one wall hangs a figure of Christ. When the flames burned down the door they charred the feet. Then the fire suddenly ceased.

A great square stone serves as the altar and on this is another much-decayed wooden statue of Saint Anne dating from the fifteenth century. Outside, a plaque on the wall reads : 'Visitors are earnestly requested to treat this chapel with respect, for within its walls on the memorable 18 June 1815, many of the brave defenders of Hougoumont passed to their rest'.

Such a notice seems unnecessary until it is remembered what happened to 'Wellington's Tree'. This stood at a crossroads on a mound and beneath its shade on that fateful day, the Duke several times halted on his horse Copenhagen to watch the fighting and issue orders. Although it survived, sightseers gradually hacked pieces of it away until only part of the trunk remained. This was purchased by an Englishman in 1818 and was carved into a chair which is now in possession of Her Majesty Queen Elizabeth II.

Entering the long main street at Waterloo you will notice a sign reading *Tombe Jambe D'Uxbridge* next to a petrol station and it means just what it says – a memorial tomb not to a famous man but to his leg! Amputations were many during and after the fighting and Lord Uxbridge's was perhaps the most celebrated of the many hundreds of legs sawn off on that dreadful day. It is related that the shot that did the damage passed over the neck of Copenhagen and Uxbridge cried out, 'By God sir,

8 *Chapel of the Holy Blood, Bruges*

I've lost my leg', and Wellington replied, 'By God sir, so you have!'

This sounds more like the truth than an alternative version sometimes quoted. In this the Duke is supposed to have exclaimed 'My God, sir, you have lost your leg', and Uxbridge to have replied, 'By God sir, so I have!' Whatever the circumstance, grape shot shattered Uxbridge's knee and he was carried off the battlefield in a blanket to a peasant's house so that the damage could be assessed. On the way he cheerfully talked about the chances of saving his limb or sawing it off.

In the kitchen of a farmhouse it was decided that the limb had to be removed. While the doctors made ready for the operation he wrote a letter to his wife and talked now and then with his staff about the fighting. He was stoic during the amputation, never flinching save to point out that the instrument did not seem very sharp – which might well have been the case for, by the end of the day, the surgeons were not only exhausted but their saws and knives blunted. When the operation was over Uxbridge's pulse rate had scarcely altered. He grinned at his ADC and remarked, 'I have had a pretty long run. I have been a beau for these 47 years, and it wouldn't be fair to cut out the young men any longer'. A brilliant cavalry officer, he was afterwards made Marquess of Anglesey. A few years later he returned to Waterloo and arranged to have dinner at the very table where his leg had been amputated.

A few weeks after the battle, Uxbridge's nieces visited the village. One of them, Miss Georgy Capel, wrote: 'The old woman showed me into the room in which he had been carried and the chair on which he sat with blood upon it. She appears to feel thoroughly the honour of having sheltered such a hero under her roof and spoke of him in a manner that would have warmed your heart. From the house we went into the pretty little garden in the centre of which the leg is interred. It was overgrown with weeds, which we cleared away. The old woman is expecting a stone from Brussels which is to be laid upon it'.

An old Baedeker describes the statue as 'absurd' but, absurd or not, it is one of the very few memorials commemorating the British contribution to victory at Waterloo. The French have done much better for posterity and the farmstead Le Caillou, Napoleon's overnight headquarters, is now a museum supported financially by the French Government and housing an excellent collection of relics.

The Napoleon legend continues to live and, on the nearest Sunday to the anniversary of the battle, a parade of enthusiasts, wearing the uniform of the Grand Armée, regularly takes place. Wellington is remembered solely by the small Wellington Museum in Waterloo's main street on the opposite side of the road to the tomb of Uxbridge's leg. The entrance is through the old post house which was the Duke's headquarters. Here you may see the various rooms much as they were long ago, bare and utilitarian plus a few framed engravings, letters, paper cuttings and mementoes which have been added. Wellington's folding oak table, with its threadbare chair does not stand properly on the uneven floor – nor is it polished. Yet here he wrote his famous dispatches and the news of victory. It is said that the evening after the battle the table had been laid for dinner for the Duke and his staff but that when he returned so many were wounded or dead that he had to feed alone. Later, wearily climbing the stairs to his austere bedchamber he found a wounded officer lying in his narrow bed and rather than disturb him that night Napoleon's conqueror lay upon the floor – and fell asleep.

3. Antwerp

You emerge from a costly palatial building, which has one of the finest marble staircases in Europe, and stand outside its Renaissance façade to stare upwards at an enormous camel on a rooftop across to your right. The animal stares back superciliously. It is said that the Moslem knows 99 names for Allah but that the camel holds his head thus because he knows the hundredth! No, you are not in Africa or Florida's Disneyland. You have just left the Baroque-style Central Station of the third greatest port in Europe, a city of art, history and diamonds – Antwerp. To one side stretches the green lawn of the Astridplein and just east of the station exit is the entrance to a most unusual zoo. The camel you see on the rooftop is stone but those in the zoo itself are real enough and wander freely as if in a safari park. Large exotic birds are not caged in because the ingenious use of bright lights dissuades them from flying away. In the reptile house many of the reptiles are free for cold currents of air stop them from roaming.

Even if you do not come to Antwerp by train the Central Station is a good place from which to begin an interesting tour to the Market Square by foot and, if you have patience, you can usually find somewhere to park your car. Before you is a wide bustling street with vivid neon signs, hotels, trams, taxis and inviting-looking stores. It is the Keyserlei, the main shopping street which has innumerable little cafés offering a cup of coffee or a glass of wine if you wish to rest while sightseeing, many of them attractively jutting out on to the pavement, glassed in during the winter months and open in the summer. Within a few minutes' walk the street name changes to Teniersplaats which is lined with neo-classical buildings, one being the opera house. Number 50 was the former Royal Palace and is now the International Culture Centre. Its façade is very ornate with gilded statues. Neptune holds his trident high above the shoppers and passers-by while Mercury looks as if he will fly away on winged feet above the crowds at any moment.

Teniersplaats merges into Leysstraat which in turn widens into Meir, the city's commercial centre with office buildings, banks, boutiques, food and chocolate shops with attractive window displays and huge departmental stores like 'Innovation'.

If you take a narrow street to the left named Rubensstraat you will find the painter's famous house at number 9. It looks unprepossessing outside but it is one of the most delightful patrician dwellings in Antwerp.

Peter Paul Rubens' House was built by the artist in 1613-17 in Flemish Renaissance style. As you step in through the front entrance from the street you find yourself facing a surprisingly beautiful courtyard with portico in flamboyant Baroque vein, beyond which is a garden. Trees and shrubs are clipped in ornamental shapes and tiny box hedges hem in pocket handkerchief-sized green lawns with flower beds and urns. The house itself is equally delightful and became the property of the city of Antwerp on 1 August 1937. Like seventeenth-century Dutch mansions the flooring is often of black and white flagstones, the walls of gilded leather and the leaded windows of tiny diamond-shaped panes. Room leads into room through delicately carved wooden doorways. A shallow wooden staircase winds upstairs where the windows give views over the garden. The Art Gallery on the ground floor is hung with paintings and at one end are busts of Caesar, Vitellius, Aetius, Cicero, Hercules and Seneca set in small niches. The rest of the house and the spacious studio have retained their former charm and the walls are covered with Rubens' paintings and works by his pupils and colleagues. Important acquisitions have been added from time to time including two portraits of the artist's grandparents. Chamber music concerts are held in the Rubens' House once or twice a week during the winter months, under the auspices of the 'Friends of Rubens' House' who are also responsible for many of the treasures which furnish the rooms.

Rubens led a life that many an artist would envy. He was born in Siegem, Westphalia, the son of an Antwerp lawyer Jan Rubens. He studied painting in Antwerp under Tobias Verhaecht, Adam van Noort and Otto Venius, and was later admitted as a master to the city's Painters' Guild of Saint Luke. He then studied in Italy and Spain for eight years and when he returned home in 1609 he was appointed court painter to the Archdukes and Regents of Belgium.

In 1604 Rubens married Isabella Brant in Antwerp and there are several paintings of this graceful young woman in the artist's early paintings. He was commissioned to paint many of the important pictures that we see today in Antwerp's Cathedral and churches. He accepted many commissions abroad and Marie de Medici invited him to do the decorative panels of the 'Galerie de Luxembourg' which he completed in Paris. After 17 years of marriage Isabella died and Rubens returned to Spain to work for Philip IV. Later he was knighted by Charles I of England and he went as ambassador to the court of Saint James. Rubens returned to Antwerp in 1630 and married young Helene Fourment who, like his first wife, acted as his model in many of his paintings.

Rubens' services were required in 1635 when Ferdinand of Austria became ruler of the Netherlands government on the death of his aunt. He decorated the streets of Antwerp with triumphal arches and 'spectacula' said not to have been equalled before. Sketches of these are still preserved in Antwerp, St Petersburg, Cambridge and Windsor.

The Flemish school of painting never found a successor to Rubens. None of his four sons became an artist although, according to his will, his drawings were to belong to any one of his sons who might become a painter or, in the event of one of his daughters marrying a celebrated artist, they were to be her portion. The valuable collection was dispersed and of the pictures sold, many went to Spain. Yet, because he was so prolific, his paintings can be seen and enjoyed not only in Belgium but throughout the important galleries in the world.

Rubens' House is open to the public free of charge every day except Monday from 10 a.m. to 5 p.m. and conducted visits can be arranged.

When you leave Rubens' House a short distance to the left takes you to the New Theatre. If you walk along the Schuttershofstraat, a narrow street where the stepped house façades have been well restored, you come to Lange Gasthuisstraat. Number 19 is the Mayer Van den Bergh Museum, a mansion owned by a merchant family of that name who gave it as a museum when their son was killed in a riding accident. It has many important paintings, sculptures, illuminated manuscripts, plaquettes, glass paintings, bronzes, tapestries and furniture. Of these the most interesting item is 'Mad Meg' a painting by Pieter Breughel the Elder. This was bought by Fritz Mayer Van den Bergh at an auction in Cologne in 1897. It cost 390 German marks because it was so badly displayed above other paintings that no one noticed it and a ladder was needed to see it properly! It was well worth the climb. The picture has held a leading place in the collection of the Emperor Rudolph II of Czechoslovakia. It was purloined by the Swedes when they plundered Prague in 1648 and became part of the collection of Queen Christine of Sweden. It is uncertain, but would be interesting to know, how it ended up in the Cologne auction.

It is always advisable to check when museums open if you particularly wish to visit one. Times differ not only in summer and winter but from place to place and are constantly changed. The Mayer Van den Bergh museum is generally open during the summer (May to September) from 10 a.m. to 5 p.m. every day except Monday. In winter (October to April) it is open at the same times on even days of the month except Mondays.

Number 33 in the same street is yet another small museum

known as the 'Maidens' House' because it was once a girls'
orphanage. The fine façade of this sixteenth-century house is
striking in that above the gate there is a bas relief which shows
girls in their classrooms on one side while on the other children
wait for admission at the entrance. Above this Christ is en-
throned with outstretched arms while over His head is a pelican
– a symbol of charity.

The rooms on the ground floor at the front of the building
have several interesting exhibits including rare Antwerp pottery
in the form of porridge basins of the sixteenth century. The
Maidens' Orphanage not only houses a museum and a quiet
little cobbled courtyard with statues of a Virgin and Child in
one corner, but also functions as the administrative offices of the
Public Assistance Board. I walked into one office by mistake but
no one seemed to mind. It seems strange when you leave this
quiet place to find the whole street is full of banks! If you take
the Boogkeersstraat opposite and turn right along Vleminckveld
and Kammenstraat which leads into Oude Koornmarkt, you
will again see many sixteenth- and seventeenth-century houses.
You pass by a sixteenth-century passageway, Vlaeykensgang, and
find yourself at the end of your walk in the Market Square with
its beautiful Town Hall, handsome Guild Houses and the Brabo
fountain. Quieter, less animated than its more famous counterpart in Brussels, the Grand' Place is an attractive place to rest
over a drink.

The Town Hall has been partially destroyed and rebuilt
several times yet behind its Renaissance façade it has a sumptuous
interior with frescoes by Leys, Lagye, de Jans and others and
paintings by nineteenth- and twentieth-century artists. The Leys
room is where the Burgomaster and the Aldermen meet to dis-
cuss the administration of the city. The old State Room is now
the Wedding Room where the Greek-like caryatids by Cornelis
Floris have been restored by Raphael Paladanus. Victor Lagye of
Ghent did the interesting frescoes which show wedding fashions of
various periods of history. Queen Victoria was received at the
Town Hall in 1834 and Queen Elizabeth II in 1966. The Town

Hall can be visited on Tuesdays, Fridays and Saturdays from noon to 3.30 p.m. and on other days from 8.30 to 3.30 when you can see the Gallery, the Council Chamber and the Militia Room. The last named has a map which shows where some 10,000 bombs and rockets landed during the Second World War, a silent witness of Antwerp's agony during those dreadful days.

The writing desk of the Burgomaster is made of wood from the 'Tree of Liberty' which used to grow in the Market Square. It is now replaced by the Brabo fountain which symbolizes the liberty of Antwerp.

Legend ascribes the name of Antwerp to 'Hand Werpen' ('throw the hand') in connection with Antigonus, a giant, who had the frightening habit of cutting off the right hand of ships' captains who refused to pay his exorbitant tolls when sailing up the Scheldt. These amounted to half the value of the cargo. The hands were thrown over the town ramparts into the Scheldt, *pour encourager les autres.* Salvius Brabo, who acted as a Saint George killing the dragon, slew the almighty Antigonus and has been venerated through the centuries. Two hands still appear in the coat of arms of the city and the Brabo fountain is a lasting reminder of a brave man who did not fear the great strength of Antigonus the giant. Legend the story may be, but who can resist a Belgian David facing a Goliath? The fountain is a graceful one with maidens, a seal and other sea creatures cavorting under the splashing water while Brabo races along the top, handsome as a Greek God, his right hand held high clasping the giant's severed hand. The only false note is that Brabo is supposed to be about to throw the giant's hand into the Scheldt but has his back to the river. Yet perhaps this is poetic licence because in this attitude the hero poses against the finely carved tracery work of the Town Hall and it has never been known for a photographer to argue the point.

The space in front of the Town Hall is a vantage place to see the elaborate open-work of Notre Dame Cathedral spire from a short distance. Charles v used to say that this elegant specimen of Gothic architecture built in 1352-3 ought to be preserved in a case and Napoleon compared it to a piece of Mechelen lace. It is particularly beautiful on a sunny day when the tracery work is etched against a blue sky.

Notre Dame Cathedral faces Groenplaats on the south side, a busy square with a bronze statue of Rubens in the centre on top of a pedestal 20 feet high. It was erected in 1840 and at the master's feet lie the symbols of his lifetime pursuits. Brush, palette and hat denote the artist, scrolls and books the statesman and diplomat.

The cathedral is the largest and one of the most lovely Gothic churches in Belgium. The interior has triple aisles with vaulting soaring up to 130 feet supported by 125 pillars. It has been muti-lated terribly in the past and several times restored. It has known glorious occasions such as one in 1555 when Philip of Spain held a chapter of the Golden Fleece there attended by the Emperor Charles and eight kings. The value of its paintings is inestimable and include three Rubens. The most famous of the latter is in the south transept, the 'Descent from the Cross', a commission from the Guild of Antwerp archers. Particularly poignant is the utter inertness of Jesus and the tender handling of the body. These Rubens' masterpieces were looted by the French and later returned to Antwerp by Louis XVIII at the request of the Duke of Wellington.

Before the west front of Notre Dame Cathedral you can see an old well which has an exquisite wrought iron canopy topped by another slender statue of Salvius Brabo. The artist was Quentin Metsys, a gifted blacksmith who also became a famous painter.

Quentin Metsys' story is a romantic one. He came from Leuven to seek his fortune in Antwerp where he became enamoured of the daughter of a well-known painter. The girl returned his love but the father refused to give his consent to the young couple's marriage, saying that a blacksmith was not good enough for his only child.

One day Quentin was visiting the girl and wandered into her father's studio. A portrait had been left on an easel to dry and

Quentin idly picked up a brush and with quick strokes painted a little fly on the canvas. When the girl's father returned he tried to brush the fly off the canvas with his hand but could not do so. He looked closer and asked his daughter who had painted the perfect little fly.

'Quentin Metsys', she replied proudly.

'This youth is no mere blacksmith', cried the father, 'you have my permission to marry such a gifted painter'.

Metsys started to paint, although he did not give up his superb metal work, and did so brilliantly and became so successful that he was one of the artists who helped raise the status of the Antwerp school of painting to that of Bruges and Ghent.

Quentin Metsys painted a 'Pietà' in 1508 which became an altar-piece in the Cathedral. It is a scene before the entombment of Christ with Joseph of Arimathaea tenderly removing the remains of thorns from Christ's forehead. The two Marys are grief stricken. One holds Jesus' foot as if to warm it. The pathos is such that this is believed to be Metsys' greatest work. Today it is in the Royal Museum of Fine Arts, Leopold de Waelplaats. This museum, built in neo-Classical style at the turn of the century, is a treasure trove and has over 1,000 works of old masters including a number of Flemish primitives. It is opened every day except Monday from 10 a.m. till :

3 p.m. from 1st January till 31st January
4 p.m. from 1st February till 14th April
5 p.m. from 15th April till 30th September
4 p.m. from 1st October till 14th November
3 p.m. from 15th November till 31st December

Closed : 1st January, 1st May, Ascension Day and Christmas Day

Entrance Price : 5 francs

Free Sundays and Bank Holiday; Wednesday and Saturday from 1 p.m.

I am very fond of this museum for two reasons apart from the beautiful works it contains. One, which is so important to visitors, is that all the best-known and famous pictures are in 12 galleries on the first floor so that, if you have little time to spare, you can go to these straight away and not wander from gallery to gallery trying to find your particular favourites. Secondly, the entrance has an excellent postcard and book stall which is spread out so that you are in nobody's way if you wish to examine the cards and colour slides.

In the first 12 rooms of Antwerp's Fine Arts Museum each visitor will have favourites to see. In room 2 Jean de Candida's portrait by Hans Memling draws admirers. Not only is the young man stern and handsome but he has a dimple in his chin and his brown eyes look at you inquiringly. A scull cap is perched on his black curly hair and for some reason he holds up a coin in his left hand for you to study. There are three other Memlings in this room all depicting heavenly choirs. In one, Christ is flanked by singing angels. The other two are of angel orchestras one with harp, violin and flutes, the other with more reed instruments and a mandolin.

Room 3 has Quentin Metsys' 'Piéta' and Jean Fouquet's strangely modern 'Virgin and Child'. Mary, with pearl-decorated open crown and blue-grey robe with the left breast exposed, has an ermine cape around her nacreous bare shoulders. The Christ Child, held by an angel, is surprisingly large and straight backed. He gazes ahead with purpose.

Lucas Cranach's 'Eve' holds court in room 4. Her golden hair falls below her hips, her unclothed body is faintly golden with rosy undertones. She holds such an appetizing reddish apple in her right hand that you could pluck it from the canvas before the snake, poised to attack, lowers his jaws to do the same thing.

There is a painting by Pieter Breughel III in the same room with the three wise kings coming to worship Christ in the stable. They wear their exotic robes and crowns yet the rustic scene is Belgium in wintertime. Snow covers the ground and farm rooftops. Foraging dogs search beneath bare trees. It is fascinating how Breughel set his Middle East religious themes in Flemish backgrounds. Yet for his viewers, who never travelled it was natural for this was the way they visualized the Christian stories.

Rubens' 'L'enfant Prodigue' shows another rustic scene in Room 5. There is a lackadaisical, end-of-the-day atmosphere. Poetic licence allows the onlooker to see inside a barn where cows are patiently waiting to be milked and horses rest after the day's harvesting. At the same time, outside the barn, the prodigal is telling his adventures to a plump farm girl in the lingering light. It is the time of day when the sky is still blue but sunset is just touching the horizon. The girl is tipping a vat of swill into a stone trough while pigs and piglets wait impatiently. Birds fly low in the evening light to their nests. The breeze has ceased so that even the trees are still. It is that magic moment at evening when the day's labour is finished.

Of the many museums in Antwerp, four are probably unique. The Plantin Moretus with its history of printing; the Steen, the national maritime museum; the Butcher's Hall with its gallery of musical instruments and harpsichords, and the Sterckshof with its unusual section 'The Diamond'.

Diamonds may be a girl's best friend but are also one of Antwerp's. The city has a 500-year old tradition of diamond cutting, its own diamond bourse and is one of the world's largest diamond centres. It is not difficult to know why these gems have an enduring glamour. A diamond never deteriorates and will be just as beautiful generations hence as it is today and certainly appreciates in value. They are probably the most portable form of wealth and easily concealed in the event of a crisis. Because of their value and scintillating beauty as an adornment, they are prized above all other gems.

Stories about the world's leading diamonds always make the headlines whether it is the Cullinan, now in the British Crown, the gem Elizabeth Taylor has in a ring or the yellow stone recently picked up in Kimberley which has turned out to be the world's ninth largest diamond weighing 616 carats.

Luck as much as anything else is the greatest asset when mining diamonds. They are always found in single crystals, not attached to any matrix and each is individual. Although they continue to be mined the demand is greater than ever and the smaller ones play an increasing part in modern industry. Because of its hardness the stone can only be ground and polished with its own powder and cutting and cleaving have to be discussed and worked out carefully. Such skill is required that, if a master cleaver misjudges the right place by a hair's breadth, the result could be shattered worthless remains. However large the stone or beautiful the colour a diamond's value cannot be assessed until it has been cut and polished and then the four 'Cs' must be judged – carat weight, cut, clarity and colour. Modern techniques of cutting allow as much as 90 per cent of the light entering the stone to leave it again. It is in the application of each skill that Antwerp comes into the picture for, since the fourteenth century, diamond cutting has been as much a part of the Antwerp scene as the ancient port itself.

I went to a diamond exhibition in Antwerp in 1973 which was enthralling. Each firm had a showcase with different designs. In one, dolls represented a bride and groom. The bride's headdress was in diamonds, also her veil and bouquet. The groom was handing her a diamond ring. Written on black velvet in diamonds at their feet were the words 'A diamond is forever'. Another case displayed a snowcapped mountain studded with shining diamonds and a tiny explorer holding up one in his hand. Yet another was a model of the world studded with differently coloured stones. The colours varied but I only saw one rose-coloured diamond and was told that they are extremely rare.

As I was leaving the exhibition I was given a little booklet about the care of diamonds and on one page there were a number of 'Do's and Don'ts'. It pointed out that they lose their sparkle if dirty, can be chipped by carelessness or lost from a loosened setting. As a cleaning bath it suggested a tablespoon of household ammonia and a few soapflakes whisked into two cups of warm water. Swish the diamonds gently in the solution and scrub lightly with a little eyebrow brush. Rinse in lukewarm water, dip in surgical spirit to remove any remaining soap film and drain on a tissue. The three 'don'ts' were as follows :

Don't wear your diamond ring when you wash your hands, apply cosmetics, do the dishes, or dig in the garden. Soap, creams, powder and dirt will all dim the brilliance. A good plan when washing your hands in a public wash room is to hold your ring between your teeth; that way you won't lose it.

Don't bang your diamond against a hard surface. There's not much chance you will hit it hard enough to chip or crack the stone – but there's no reason to take even that chance.

Don't, when you have several diamond pieces, jumble them together in your drawer or jewellery case. Although the diamond is the hardest substance known and cannot wear out, one diamond can scratch another. Either wrap them in tissue or keep them in separate boxes.

The Plantin Moretus Museum of Printing, in 1549 the home of the celebrated printer Christopher Plantin, is world renowned. Christopher Plantin first worked as a bookbinder but one night, while carrying a tooled leather casket he had made for King Philip of Spain to hold a piece of jewellery, he was set upon by footpads who mistook him for somebody else. He sustained such injuries he could never work on leather again but, fortunately for mankind, he switched to printing.

A visit to the mansion of Plantin, later known as Plantin-Moretus (the added name being that of the founder's son-in-law), is a must for those interested in any aspect of the printed word. This gracious, patrician house has been owned by the same family and used for printing from 1555 until it was sold to the city of Antwerp in 1876 by Edward John Hyacinthe Moretus. The building has had many narrow escapes, the most dangerous being from one of Hitler's V-2 rockets which caused much damage but only to the fabric of the building, which has since been restored.

On the ground floor there is a proof-readers' room and the original printing office with its types and presses. Living quarters have spacious rooms with wooden beamed ceilings, parquet floors and walls of tooled Flemish and Spanish leather. Portraits include some by Rubens who was a regular guest, as were other eminent artists and scholars down through the years. Several 'wings' enclose a quiet formal garden with lawns and box hedges. The southern one and part of the western one were erected in the sixteenth century and the others were added later.

From 1570 Plantin was appointed typographer-in-chief to Philip II of Spain which gave him the monopoly of the sale of liturgical books, missals, breviaries and psalm books and the house contained no less than 22 printing presses.

The upper floor has the family library, a music room with a harpsichord, an elaborate sitting room and an eighteenth-century room lined with Pompadour leather. You can look down into the garden through leaded windows as well as gaze at antique furniture, priceless manuscripts, first editions, and engravings. The most interesting spot upstairs is the workshop or type foundry with its stone flooring, woodblocks, copper plates and glass cases full of fascinating printing devices and international types of lettering.

The 'Butchers' Hall' in the centre of old Antwerp near the Town Hall is sixteenth-century Gothic in style and built of alternating layers of red and white sandstone. Because it has been recently cleaned it is popularly known as 'Rashers of Bacon'. The Butchers' Guild commissioned one of the architects of Antwerp Cathedral, H. de Waghemakere, to design the building. The large open-space ground floor was used to sell meat and the upper floors contained a Guild Chamber, a chapel, banqueting hall and kitchen.

The Guild was a close-knit community and families intermarried. The Butchers' Hall was both a centre for work and pleasure and it was not until the French Revolution, when craft guilds were abolished, that it lost its *raison d'etre*. Today the building houses all types of museum exhibits including armour, furniture, ship's figureheads and diamond working tools. Other items include a lavishly decorated sarcophagus containing the Mummy of an Egyptian temple musician of the 21st dynasty and models of famous diamonds.

A drawback to the Butchers' Hall having been turned into a

9 *The Gothic belfry at Bruges*

museum is that the only access to the upper storeys is by two spiral staircases so narrow that passing is virtually impossible. The authorities have wisely instituted a one-way traffic scheme. When I climbed the stairway I could hear music in the distance and as I went around the last curve and came out into the gallery I saw someone playing a harpsichord. The music was so beautiful that I knew it was practice for a concert. The player was so intent that she did not see me and I did not dare ask if the concert was to take place there. I can think of no better setting.

The entrance and exit to the Butchers' Hall is on the east side and the square before it is edged with stepped gabled buildings. Number 16 was where Sir Thomas More stayed while in Antwerp and it was here that he entertained Erasmus and discussed his ideas for *Utopia*. English wool merchants lived at number 30 in the sixteenth century when the house was known as 'The Shield of London'. If you stand in the centre of the space before the Butchers' Hall and look at the skyline on the right with the hall behind you, you can see a bronze horse apparently climbing the step gables of one of the old houses. This illusion is dispelled if you walk further back and you will then realize the horse is part of a team pulling a chariot on a building further away. The illusion makes a good photograph!

To visit the 'Steen' museum from here you walk towards the river. On the way you will probably pass through the Red Light district where ladies in various stages of dress and undress pose in the windows. Their ages are as varied as the colour of their hair and their weight. They pass their spare time knitting, sewing, reading, eating or just staring into space.

The Steen Maritime museum was opened on the 17 May 1935 by Prince Albert of Belgium. It is an ancient grey stronghold, a type of gatehouse with step gables and towers like those in a Hans Christian Andersen fairy tale. Built on a promontory it juts out over the River Scheldt and is the perfect setting for such a museum. Each of the 13 rooms, leading from one to the other or connected by winding staircases, contains its own collection and their names give you some idea of the contents. 'Seamen's customs', 'Pleasure', 'Inland Navigation', 'The Development of the Ship', 'Belgium Maritime History' and so on. One room deals with ship decorating. The most popular exhibits are undoubtedly ship models. One is of a three-masted galleon of the eighteenth century and a recent acquisition is of the English three-decked *Caledonia*. There is also a comprehensive library with some 10,000 volumes which is open to anyone who is interested in the different aspects of maritime life. Like the other municipal museums in Antwerp the 'Steen' is opened every day, except Mondays, from 10 a.m. to 5 p.m. and admission is free.

Inevitably after you leave the 'Steen' you gravitate to the waterfront. Ships line the quays and there is an elevated promenade on top of the quayside warehouses which is particularly enticing at sunset. It leads to a bridge, a marvellous vantage point for photographers, and a chance to look along the placid Scheldt. An old Antwerp saying goes that 'Antwerp has to thank God for the Scheldt and the Scheldt for all the rest'. 'The rest' continues to grow. The port itself has been thrust eight miles downstream to the world's largest lock – Zandvliet. Tracts of land along the river have been eagerly bought by Canadian and American companies as well as local ones. The Kennedy tunnel, its five concrete sections prefabricated then sunk into the river bed and joined together, was opened in 1969 and handles both rail and road traffic. A fast pleasureboat trip is the best way to see the port and on your return journey you get a wonderful overall view of the city skyline, its focal point being the Gothic splendour of the cathedral tower.

4. Food and Drink

Eating and slimming simply do not go together in Belgium unless you have great will power. Belgian food is delicious but extremely rich and its skilful cooks are such masters of the art that the very aromas are enticing enough to make you forget your waistline. No wonder, when you consider that the chef combines the best of Flemish, Walloon and French cuisine. One way out of the difficulty on a visit to Belgium, which helps both purse and waistline, is to have just one full meal a day but try to make it dinner rather than lunch if you can. This arrangement with a Continental breakfast and a light snack at lunchtime will give most people all the calories they need.

The gastronomic range is enormous and Belgians are not afraid of experimenting with food, so the only answer is when in Belgium do what the Belgian does. He reckons that good food constitutes one of the truly great interests in life – and who is to say he is wrong? It is difficult to know which speciality to try first because there are so many but no dissertation on Belgian food can overlook Belgium's own particular vegetable *witloof*. We call it 'chicory', the French 'endive' but whatever the name the Belgians discovered it and cook it in various delicious ways.

Witloof (whiteleaf) has modest beginnings. Its story begins in the middle of the previous century. Towards the year 1850, the people in the outlying villages of the Brussels area, which have now become part of the Belgian capital, depended almost entirely for a living on moderately successful market gardening. In addition to potatoes, wheat and manglewurzle, the peasants in this area used to grow vegetable roots from which they extracted a coffee substitute known as chicory; this was in fairly wide use, for coffee was then an expensive import from distant lands. The roots were taken for drying to small factories, but the peasants used to keep for themselves those of the roots that were too small to be processed. One year, during a particularly mild winter, the roots that had been left in a heap next to a barn began to germinate. They grew long shoots with small yellow-white leaves. At the end of the winter when fresh vegetables were at a premium, some of the growers took these leaves and shoots to the market in Brussels, where they managed to sell them under the picturesque appellation of *barbe de capucin* (friar's beard) or *pissenlit* (dandelion).

Witloof is today a much improved version of the chicory shoots. Experiments were carried out on the plants in Brussels Botanical Garden and it was soon discovered that the heart of the plant should be kept warm, damp and dark. Soon *witloof* came to be known as 'Brussels chicory' and to be grown in most of the villages around the city. It became the speciality of family concerns in the area between Brussels, Malines and Louvain, in the very heart of Belgium. The reason for this was that the *witloof* needs a light, half-sandy, half-clayey soil, which can be found in this particular area. Since then chicory growing has spread to other parts of Belgium too and nowadays some 13,000 families live solely by this crop. As it calls for constant care and attention, it is still grown almost entirely by small concerns. Even so, production amounts to some 100,000 tons a year, and the area under cultivation covers more than 22,000 acres. Harvesting still has to be done by hand, root by root. Cut at the top of the root, the vegetable is then stripped of its outer leaves in lukewarm water and dried.

Most salads nowadays contain raw chicory and it readily lends itself to a variety of dishes. Gourmets and hostesses are using it more and more. Small chunks are sometimes used instead of squares of toast for cocktail appetizers. Dishes include *witloof a l'anglaise, witloof a la suisse,* a 'provencal salad', *witloof royal,* and, in an even more poetic strain, there is *'witloof Annabella'*, 'Danish Christmas Salad', and 'Reducer's Delight'. There is also a fish salad in which small slices of raw *witloof* are served with herrings and shrimps. There is another reason why *witloof* has become so popular : though rich in vitamins B1, B2 and C it only contains 47 calories to the lb. For those who want to keep an eye on their figures and favour a low-calory diet this outstanding vegetable can add taste and variety to an otherwise insipid diet.

Very strict regulations have been introduced in Belgium to maintain the quality of *witloof,* and standards for export have been laid down by government decree.

I find the easiest way to serve chicory is to slice the heads and place them in a frying pan with a little butter, ground pepper, pinch of salt and a lump of sugar. The latter takes away any bitter taste. Put on the lowest possible heat while the butter melts taking care not to burn until the chicory's own juice appears. Cover the pan and then let the mixture simmer for about ten minutes or until a fork can pierce through the chicory easily. If you wish, a dash of lemon juice guards the appetizing white colour. Chicory served this way as an extra vegetable is delicious.

Chicory heads can be stuffed with chopped meat, tied with string or even rolled in breadcrumbs and placed in the oven with a slice of ham, or bacon, to cook. It is often served like this in restaurants. Sometimes white sauce and cheese are added.

Perhaps the best known Belgian vegetable is Brussel sprouts. It is frequently ruined by being just boiled unimaginatively, but in Belgium they have better ways. After boiling in salted water until tender, it is browned in melted butter or pork dripping. Or again it is mashed and seasoned with nutmeg.

Jets de houblon is a vegetable with a delectable flavour rather like asparagus and is only available in Belgium in the spring. It consists of tender hop plant shoots which can be bought pre-cleaned from the greengrocers. These have to be washed in water then thrown in boiling water with salt and lemon added. When the hops are tender they are served with mousseline sauce and poached eggs or with butter or cream accompanying meat. These little hops can also be served fresh with salads.

One other special vegetable dish that should be mentioned is 'Malines Asparagus Soufflé' which is easy to prepare. After having removed the hard ends place the spears in a small amount of melted butter and a chopped onion before cooking them in salt water. Boil and then dry. Serve with a sauce of melted butter, hard boiled eggs and finely chopped parsley. Each person prepares his own sauce by crushing the egg yolk in the butter and sprinkling it with salt and pepper.

Tomatoes are not only served in salads but are stuffed or cooked in different ways. An easy dish to prepare is '*Tomates Farcies du Littoral*'. Dip the tomatoes in boiling water so that they are easy to peel. Then cut in halves, remove the juice and the pips, season with salt and pepper and place on a round plate. Mince fillets of boiled fish with a small dessert spoon of tomato purée, 1 dessert spoon mayonnaise, 1 dessert spoon mustard and mix well. Fill the tomatoes forming a slight dome. Cover with mayonnaise and stick peeled shrimps on top. Serve with watercress.

As a 'starter' to a meal tomatoes are sometimes stuffed with shrimps mixed in mayonnaise. Belgian shrimps are small and pale pink and are at their most succulent when deep fried in a rissole mixture called *Croquette aux Crevettes,* which is also an excellent 'starter'.

The sea coast offers plenty of fish and the most famous sea food is mussels which are often served *à la marinière* or '*Le Complet Bruxellois*'. In the latter way they are accompanied by crispy potato chips. A piece of celery and an onion are minced together and cooked in a covered pan in a little butter for about 10 minutes. After rinsing a few times, about two pounds of mussels are added with a pinch of salt, ground pepper and the juice of half a lemon. This is cooked in the covered pan for another 10 minutes. By then the mussels should have completely opened. Before serving add chopped parsley to the juice and pour on the mussels.

The well known dish *anguilles au vert* – green eels – originally came from Antwerp but can be ordered anywhere in Belgium. Recipes are many but this one by Gaston Clement, master of the art, is not too difficult and is as follows :

Choose average-sized eels, clean them well, skin them, cut off their heads, tails and fins and then section them. For about 2 pounds of fish mince together a handful of sorrel and one including sage, citronelle (a leaf with a lemon flavour) and a large quantity of chervil. Put 50 grams of butter and two chopped shallots in a pan to heat and then add the eels. Stir while cooking for a few minutes, add three-quarters of a litre of white wine and water to cover the fish as well as the herbs. Season and cook for 10 minutes. Meanwhile put the juice of one lemon, two yolks of egg and one teaspoon cornflour into a salad bowl. Stir quickly while pouring the contents of the pan into the salad bowl. This exquisite dish is served hot or cold according to individual taste.

Of the game dishes of the Ardennes '*Porc à la Saint Hubert*' is very good especially when wild boar cutlets or chops are used. This method is easy to follow. Put the chops in an earthenware dish, add thyme, bay, a sprig of parsley, freshly-ground pepper, a pinch of ground nutmeg, a sliced clove of garlic and pour one large glass of red wine and 1 spoon of olive oil over all. Let this marinate for two days. Remove chops, season them and cook in butter. Put them in a dish and keep warm. Let the sauce evaporate until the desired quantity is attained and then add 1 dessert spoon of mustard, 1 dessert spoon of red currant jelly, and a dash of tarragon vinegar. Put some cornflour in a few drops of cold water and pour while stirring it into the sauce until thickened. Try the seasoning, strain and add a piece of butter to finish. Pour some of the sauce on the chops and put the rest in a sauce boat. Serve together with chestnut mash, chestnut croquettes or buttered lentils.

Cooking in southern Belgium has the reputation of being particularly rich and varied. This may be the result not only of proximity to France but a reflection of Spanish influence in the past. Other parts of the country have many dishes in common with Holland and Luxembourg though some are prepared and seasoned differently.

Smoked ham, not unlike Parma ham to the taste, is also a speciality of the Ardennes. It is served in paper-thin slices. This region also boasts pork, goose and wild boar patés. These can sometimes be found in Britain in delicatessens packed in attractive earthenware bowls.

Bruges is well known for '*Carbonnade à la Flamande*', a beef stew cooked in the local beer; Ghent for '*Waterzooi de poulet*' consisting of chicken or goose boiled in an aromatic broth served in soup plates with bread and butter and boiled potatoes as a vegetable.

Boudin sausage is a national dish, the *Boudin blanc* being the one usually preferred by visitors as the *Boudin noir* is very rich indeed. Both are served with grapes in the Ardennes but with apple sauce in most other places.

As has been mentioned already, the Belgian 'fights for his beefsteak'. This came out strongly in 1958 when a proposal was mooted to cut through a part of the centre of Brussels to improve access to the Grand Place. This would have meant destroying numerous cafés and restaurants, indeed the gastronomic centre of the city with more than 100 eating houses. The local people rebelled, fought the project and the government was obliged to issue a Royal Decree in 1960 which established the zone as a 'Sacred Island' which would be preserved and known as the Free City of Brussels. It covers five streets: Rue des Bouchers, Rue des Dominicains, Petite Rue des Bouchers, Rue Gretry and Rue de la Fourche plus the ancient Arcade the Galeries Royales Saint Hubert.

This tiny enclave, a city within a city, has its own folklore, if not municipal administration, with a town council and Burgomaster whose aim is to bring new life into the quarter. When you consider that it has more inns, restaurants, bars, taverns and dance halls than most other parts of Brussels, who knows where this might lead?

Belgian breads, pastries and sweets are numerous and have unfamiliar names but the following list covers the ones you will meet on most menu cards :

Baulus – these are to be found in all cake shop windows. They are a popular type of brioche, made with grapes and other preserved fruits and with honey on top.

Bebelutes – a kind of soft butter caramel, the work of experienced confectioners and sold especially at the seaside.

Cramique – sliced bread containing eggs, milk, sugar and sometimes dried raisins, described as a national delicacy which is very nourishing !

Craqueline – a variety of Cramique which tends towards the brioche by its composition and form but is topped with granulated sugar and is split on one side so that part of the bread, or a very thin crust, is visible.

Flan – a kind of rich, plain-based pudding. The ingredients are : 1 litre boiling milk, 200 grams sugar, orange flavouring, vanilla, cinnamon or a dash of lemon, which makes the filling, then 5 eggs, 125 grams flour, 1 spoon cold milk are mixed in an earthenware dish and the sweetened milk is poured over it. It is put in a pie dish and then cooked in the oven for 20-25 minutes.

Gaufres – Waffles which are served everywhere in Belgium and are as popular for both grown-ups and children as hot dogs are in America.

Gozette – rather similar to an apple turnover. Apricots as well as rhubarb purée or apples are used to fill them.

Mosques de Gand and Noeuda de Bruges – delicious titbits, the secret recipes for which are carefully guarded by the confectioners of Ghent and Bruges.

Pain à la Gracht – a rectangular, thin and very crisp sweet biscuit. It is made of milk, flour, yeast, butter, brown sugar, eggs, cinnamon and salt.

Pistolets – small round rolls with a split in the middle where water in the paste is replaced by milk.

Rombosse – baked apple with a sugar-based filling.

Tarte au Maton – a rich and tasty cake made of white cheese
and almonds. It is from Grammont and mainly eaten on
feast days.

All these pies, desserts and delicacies only represent an imper-
fect summary of what the gastronomical traditions of Belgium
have to offer those with a sweet tooth.

Beer is the customary daily drink for the average Belgian.
Nearly all the beers such as Stella Artois are a light lager-type
and served ice-cold. There are richer and stronger ones such as
Kriek, Lambic and Gueuze. Then there are several beers made
at monasteries such as the Guinness-like brew from Orval Abbey.
Finally, several well-known English beers can be found, as indeed
some Belgian ones are now to be had in Britain.

Cafés serving beer remain open all day and also offer wine as
well as tea and coffee but you cannot order whisky, gin or other
spirits. Wine is widely drunk but it is not produced in Belgium
itself. It has been a joke for centuries that the Belgians import
the best French wines and are as excellent connoisseurs as the
French themselves.

Although the law says you must belong to a club to drink
spirits or have them at home, it is not unusual to see waiters
fetching such drinks as whisky and soda to those who order them
in restaurants and hotels. The Belgian, in his usually charming
way, somehow manages to bend the law without breaking it!

5. East Flanders and Hainaut

Ghent, capital of East Flanders, is 32 miles north west of Brussels. Situated on the rivers Scheldt and Lys it is intersected by canals and has over 200 bridges. Although thoroughly industrialized it retains much of its medieval character and the city is proud of the fact that it has more historic buildings than Bruges or Antwerp.

Ghent and England have many links. John of Gaunt was born in the Abbey of Saint Bavo. He was fourth son of Philippa of Hainaut and Edward III of England and founded the line of Lancastrian kings – Henry IV, V and VI. Indeed, for a while he was well known in England as the heir apparent to the throne. He also acquired the title of King of Castile when he married the daughter of Peter the Cruel. Another John, John of Cleves, is a further connection with the English crown for his daughter, Anne of Cleves, had the doubtful honour of being one of Henry VIII's six wives.

Between 1764 and 1767 James Hargreaves invented the 'Spinning Jenny' whereby 16 or more threads could be spun simultaneously by one person. This was the beginning of more sophisticated methods for spinning in England. In 1805 some of the newly-invented spinning and weaving equipment was smuggled across to the Continent from England and much of this found its way to Ghent. The weaving of cotton has always flourished there and the local Cloth Hall, the meeting place of the drapers and wool merchants, is a splendid Gothic building. The cellar, happily for visitors, has been turned into an attractive café restaurant today but keeps its old world atmosphere.

Adjoining the Cloth Hall the Belfry soars skyward for some 300 feet. It is a square tower and on top of its cast iron steeple a golden dragon acts as a weathervane. It is nearly 12 feet long and, according to tradition, was brought from Constantinople (Istanbul) either by the Varangians or by the Emperor Baldwin after the Crusades. Its carillon of 52 bells includes Roland, nearly six tons in weight, a replacement for one destroyed by Charles v.

The majority of Ghent's historic buildings are floodlit from May to September and one of the most famous views is from Saint Michael's Bridge in the centre of the town. From here you can see the three great towers of Ghent ranged one behind the other. First that of Saint Nicholas's Church completed in 1250, then the Belfry with its golden dragon lending a fairytale quality and thirdly and the most impressive of all that of Saint Bavo's Cathedral.

Bavo, patron saint of Ghent, was a nobleman converted by Saint Amandus, the apostle of Flanders. As a young man he was a type of highwayman, waylaying travellers and other defenceless people and relieving them of their money and jewels. Like Saint Paul when he was converted, Bavo is said to have changed completely and he became the mildest of men – Bavo means 'mild'. He went to the forest of Mendonk where he lived in a hollow tree for seven years as a hermit. Legend has it that during this time he became so holy that the very tree flowered both summer and winter. Later a monastery was founded with his assistance by Amandus at Ghent. It was in this abbey that John of Ghent was born.

It is confusing to have Ghent spelt in so many ways. It is also written Gent and Gand; then there is John of Gaunt and to add to the complications there is a famous pun on the name. Alva the Spaniard proposed to Charles v that Ghent, which had bitterly resisted Spanish rule, should be razed to the ground. The latter replied that he could even *Mettez Paris dans son gant* – put Paris in his glove. Both men climbed on top of the belfry and there

Charles asked 'How many Spanish skins to make a glove of this size?'

The Counts of Flanders had their seat in Ghent and this was the cause of its troubled past. The first Count, Baldwin of the Iron Arm, built the castle whose magnificent shell you see today, to prevent the Normans raiding up the Scheldt. He was entrusted by Charles the Bald with defence of the northern marshes.

The castle fell in 949 and was occupied for some 50 years before the counts regained it. Once they were back in the saddle everything went well. Favoured by their castle's site on the river Lys, with the town itself at the confluence of the rivers, trade was inevitable and the cloth industry grew. Ghent reached its zenith during the thirteenth to fifteenth centuries. She could put 20,000 citizens under arms but her besetting sin was intransigence. It has been repeated down through the ages that the wealth of the burghers was only equalled by their turbulent spirit; feuds were constant, against the rival city of Bruges, against the Counts and within the guilds and the city itself. But Ghent joined forces with Bruges during the Battle of the Golden Spurs and played a conspicuous part in the long struggle of the Netherlands against Spain. It was in Ghent that a treaty, known as the Pacification of Ghent, established the league against Spanish tyranny. Here too a peace treaty was signed between Great Britain and the United States of America on 24 December 1814 – a suitable date for ceasing to fight but an unusual role for Ghent to play. It came about in this way:

In the early nineteenth century fiery disputes rose between Britain and America which nearly burst into flames several times. Quarrels at sea did not lessen when boundary lines with Canada could not be decided amicably. Finally, the American Ambassador in London declared war. It was a half-hearted affair, as, prior to this, discussions had begun to show signs of agreement. Each side had its successes and failures. The British took Washington but failed at Baltimore. Delegations of both countries met in Ghent and, after five months of negotiation, the Peace of

Ghent was signed. The following day the opponents enjoyed their Christmas dinner together.

The Castle of the Counts, which shaped the people's destiny for centuries, was built by Philip of Alsace over the site of a former one whose walls act as foundations for the present keep. Its architecture was inspired by the Crusader castles in Syria so that its reflection in the river Lys is romantic and oriental. When you go round the castle arrows numbered from 1 to 50 indicate the details and you can buy a small booklet which describes the various places.

Over the entrance between two crenellated towers there is a cross-shaped window, a rare example of its kind. The outer wall on the southern side, strengthened by 24 turrets pierced with loopholes and jutting out over buttresses, has an interior walkway. This is oval in shape and overlooks well-kept green lawns. From the top of the south west turret in the keep you can get a lovely view over the town.

The Great Hall of the keep has been the scene of many splendid occasions. On 12 November 1346, the Aldermen of Ghent came to present gifts to Count Louis de Male which included 18 pieces of cloth, 4 barrels of wine, 20 pikes and 2 oxen. In November 1445 a great banquet was given by Philip the Good, Duke of Burgundy and Count of Flanders, for the 7th chapter of the Golden Fleece. A chronicler of the time describes the food-laden banqueting table as glittering with gold vessels and tells that the backs of the chairs were hung with black velvet embroidered with the arms of Burgundy. 'The dinner lasted a long time while the trumpets and string instruments sounded', he finishes. The same author tells us that the walls were hung with priceless tapestries when Charles the Bold received the Ambassadors of the Duke of Milan in 1469.

Not such delightful scenes are brought to mind when you see the subterranean dungeons and many instruments of torture. Perhaps it is better not to remember that it was here that the awful punishment of the collar was first administered. An iron collar lined with spikes was placed tightly around the neck of the accused who was seated on a narrow stool with his limbs tied down. With the least movement the spikes pierced the skin.

Sometime between 1430 and 1480 the great cannon known as 'Dulle Griet' (Mad Meg) was manufactured. It is 17 feet long, weighs 16 tons, and fired stone balls weighing 750 pounds. Incongruously enough it is opposite the Kraanlei with its enchanting Renaissance gabled houses. It was placed here in 1578 and has remained there ever since.

Ghent's 'Great Beguinage' is the largest of its kind in the country. A Liliputian town, it has its own church and numerous tiny houses framed by low white-washed walls. Along the narrow pathways medieval doorways hide some 18 convents. Near the station there is a much smaller beguinage. At the turn of the century Ghent had 50 religious houses of various orders.

The celebrated Cathedral of Saint Bavo has some fine examples of late Gothic design in its 25 chapels despite its rather heavy exterior. It dominates the town and among its many treasures counts one of the world's great masterpieces the famous polyptych by Hubert and Jan Van Eyck, 'The Adoration of the Mystic Lamb'. It consists of a number of exquisitely painted panels.

The polyptych has been through some astonishing adventures. It nearly went to Spain for Philip II. The nude bodies of Adam and Eve offended Joseph II and were replaced by clothed figures for a time. The latter now hang near the entrance to the cathedral. The central panel vanished and reappeared in the Louvre in 1799. It was only sent back to its proper place after the Napoleonic wars. Twice German invaders have taken panels. The first time six of the side panels found their way to the King of Prussia who gave them to the Berlin museum. They came back to Belgium as reparations after the First World War. During the Second World War they went back again to Germany and were hidden. This time the Americans recovered them from salt mines in Austria and returned them.

In 1934 a panel was taken by the sacristan, who revealed before his death that it was in the luggage office at the Midi station in Brussels. There indeed one half was found, but the other was never recovered. It is a modern replacement you see today.

The composition, the first to be painted in a new oil medium, represents Christ on the judgement seat between the Virgin Mary and Saint John the Baptist listening to the songs of the angels. The Lamb of God is seen surrounded by angels, apostles, prophets, martyrs, knights and hermits on a great grassy plain studded with flowers. So minute is the detail that, if you examine each tiny blossom through a magnifying glass, it is quite perfect in shape and colour. It is not known how long Hubert spent on this work but when he died his brother Jan finished it.

In the 15th chapel, known as the Rubens although it was consecrated to Saint Peter and Saint Paul, there is a painting by the artist which shows Saint Bavo walking up steps to a monastery. He is being welcomed by Saint Amandus and the abbot. It is interesting that Saint Bavo is a self-portrait of Rubens.

Ghent is not only known for its many historic buildings but is also famed for its flowers – orchids, azaleas and begonias, particularly the latter. The discovery of this exotic blossom was not made by a Belgian but a French monk and botanist, Charles Plumier. He sailed to the Indies with Michael Begon, the Governor of San Domingo, and returned with six varieties of unknown plants which he named 'Begonias' after the leader of the expedition.

It was Louis van Houtte of Ghent who first succeeded in crossing begonia strains. Previously these flowers had single blooms but by 1872 Louis van Houtte developed the first begonia with double blooms and, from this breakthrough, more large-flowered varieties were created. In the beginning only two colours were known – red and orange – but by the turn of the century a wide range had been obtained from white to deep red, including bright red, scarlet, pink, salmon pink, orange, yellow and copper.

The flowers are grown and developed extensively throughout the area surrounding the city of Ghent. There are no less than 600 family firms whose production of about 80 million tubers a

1 Cat parade, Ypres

12 A poster showing Adolf Saxe playing his new invention

13 The River Meuse at Dinant

year is mainly exported. Starting in June, the colourful spectacle of hundreds of acres of begonias in full bloom can be seen and admired around Ghent. They continue to blossom all summer long until mid-autumn. In September a magnificent begonia carpet of gigantic dimensions covers Saint Peter's Square in such a brilliant blaze of colour that in bright sunlight you almost have to shade your eyes. The begonias are equally spectacular at night when they are illuminated. Ghent produces about half of Belgium's flowers and, once every five years, the Ghent Floralies is held in the Floralia Palace. It features thousands of exhibits from many countries and attracts a great many visitors.

If you are coming from Antwerp to Ghent a detour via Saint Nicholas, Dendermonde and Aalst makes a most pleasing drive through open countryside traversed by two rivers, the Scheldt and the Dender. Saint Nicholas is capital of the Waas country and has the largest market place in Belgium. The Count of Flanders granted a charter in 1241 and it is the most important town in East Flanders after Ghent. Its Town Hall in the square has two rooms devoted to Mercator, the famous geographer and inventor of the grid system, who was born in 1512 at Rupelmonde, not far away. Some of Mercator's maps and the navigational planisphere he invented are on display.

Dendermonde has paid dearly for its strategic position on two rivers. Normans, Spaniards, even Marlborough have used it as a battlefield and at one time, rather than have the town fall to Louis xiv, the inhabitants inundated the whole region. Yet it has several historic buildings including its Gothic church with paintings by Van Dyck and sculptures by Duquesnoy.

In East Flanders several clearly marked scenic routes have been laid out for motorists to follow. Also well worth a visit is the Puyenbroeck Provincial Park, some 1,100 acres of natural beauty which was opened in 1969.

The province of Hainaut borders East Flanders and for centuries has acted as a buffer between ambitious France and querulous Flanders. It is a mixture of smiling farmland and industry. Charleroi, on the left bank of the Sambre, is one of the centres of the coal and iron industry of Belgium. Machinery, cutlery, hardware and glass are manufactured. It was frequently besieged between the seventeenth and eighteenth centuries and passed alternatively into the hands of the Spaniards, French and Austrians. Hainaut has two historic cities – Tournai and Mons.

Tournai is about an hour's drive from Brussels. The town centre was obliterated during the last World War and only the Cathedral of Our Lady survived. It is the largest church in Belgium and one of the oldest. New buildings just off the main square are only one storey high in order not to impede the view. The belfry at the end of the main square dates from the twelfth century and is also the oldest in Belgium. At one time its carillon rang out every quarter of an hour but now it is only heard on Sundays. If you climb the 260 steps to the top the views are most impressive.

King Clovis was born in Tongres in 465 and chose Tournai as his capital and golden bees as his emblem. The tomb of his father Childeric was discovered in 1653 and contained treasure of the type usually associated with Eastern kings. This included 300 bees of pure gold which had decorated a royal mantle. These were sent to Paris to the Bibliothèque Nationale. Later Napoleon was so fascinated by them that he took golden bees as his emblem and also as a motif for his coronation robes when he was made Emperor.

The exterior of the vast Cathedral of Our Lady has whimple-like cones crowning five Romanesque towers. Inside, a very ornate Renaissance rood screen, decorated with reliefs in coloured marble, unfortunately blocks off part of the building. The reliefs, episodes from the Old and New Testaments, are somewhat amusing. One depicts a naked Jonah about to vanish into the whale's mouth. The next relief shows him coming out but with a shirt on! You must walk beyond the screen to appreciate the thirteenth-century Gothic choir. There are several paintings by Metsys, Pourbus, De Vos, Blondeel and here also is Rubens' much restored 'Souls in Purgatory'.

The Baroque pulpit is in the form of a great wooden chalice supported at the back by a carved palm tree. Palm fronds act as the baldachine.

The most fascinating things are in the treasury. Here there are ivories, manuscripts, gold and silver sacred vessels and two shrines to Our Lady and Saint Eleuthère designed by thirteenth-century goldsmiths and decorated with gems. Saint Eleuthère holds a small golden cathedral in one hand. A lovely old reliquary cross from the orient is edged with pearls and studded with jewels in unusual settings. The large Arras tapestry was woven for the cathedral choir in the fifteenth century. Perhaps most interesting for British visitors is a glass case containing a long red cape edged with gold braid which once belonged to Thomas à Becket.

Apart from the town's old buildings there is the Pont des Trous, an old three-arched stone bridge over the Scheldt. It is one of three military bridges of the thirteenth century which still exisits and, although it was bombed by the Allies during the last World War, it has since been restored.

Tournai was besieged by Henry vIII of England in 1340 who forced the ramparts at the head of 50,000 men. Later the Tudor king erected defences of which the so-called Henry vIII tower is all that remains. It is of solid masonry, not unlike the Martello towers which still remain here and there around the English coast and were built during the Napoleonic wars. Even at this time Wolsey was not far from the king's side and was appointed to the Bishopric of Tournai a few years before he became a Cardinal.

On the outskirts of Tournai at Blandain there is Le Prieuré. An attractive country residence, once an abbey, it has now been turned into a luxury hotel and is owned by Claude Gwinner and his charming wife who is an interior decorator. There are not many suites but each is different and two or three names give a clue to the décor; Lady Hamilton, the Bridal Suite and Suite of Le Petit Prince in which one wall is covered by a gorgeous organdie blue rose. Meals can be ordered according to taste and

Claude Gwinner supervises the cooking. The cellar is extensive. Le Prieuré is really a must even if you just drop in for a drink and to see the novel bar and restaurant. It stands in its own extensive grounds and such things as riding can easily be arranged.

On the N 398 Leuze-Mons road, some 15 miles before reaching Mons (45 miles south west of Brussels) you come to the 'Versailles' of Belgium, Beloeil Castle belonging to Prince Antoine of Ligne. It has been owned by the de Ligne family since the fourteenth century. Although seriously damaged by fire in 1900 when the main block was gutted, most of the furniture, paintings and tapestries were saved. Fortunately also the library escaped damage.

Inside, a double stairway leads to sumptuous State rooms, galleries and apartments. The 'Grand Salon' is embellished with gilded woodcarvings of armorial crests. Beauvais tapestries have the de Rohan arms on the fringes. The de Rohans and the Lignes were kinsmen. A large Louis xvi bureau is known as 'Talleyrand's' and the ormolu lapis lazuli clock belonged to Marie-Antoinette. Several of her personal belongings are in the 'de la Tour' salon including portraits, busts and personal mementoes. Her gifts to Prince Charles Joseph, whom she held in high esteem, are in the same salon.

When Charles de Lorraine was governor of the Low Countries he used to enjoy visiting Beloeil and there is a fine portrait of him by Mathias de Visch in the 'de Lorraine Salon'. In the small 'Salon de la Grande Catherine' there are several unusual *objets d'art* from Russia.

The 'd'Amblise' bedchamber, where walls are hung with seventeenth-century tapestries, has four delightful black lacquered writing desks with Chinoiserie decoration which belonged to Madame de Pompadour. Marking the marriage alliance between the Houses of Ligne and Orange the 'de Nassau' gallery includes rare Chinese porcelain and various curios. There are two Boulle tables from Louis xv in the 'Salon des Ambassadeurs' and three priceless Chinese porcelain vases which Catherine the Great presented to Charles Joseph de Ligne. So gallery follows gallery. The 'Medal Room' not only houses a famous numismatic collection but has several portraits of the family, some by Winterhalter.

The library is extensive and includes rare editions such as Liber Passionis with the Coat of Arms of Henry vii, an illuminated Book of Hours dedicated to Charles v in 1532, Fables de la Fontaine by Oudry and Bleau's Atlas bearing the signature of Charles of Lorraine.

The chapel, Notre Dame de Belle Dilection, not only has well-known paintings but also Limoges enamels, a superb collection of corals and fourteenth-century English alabasters.

Perhaps a saying of the eighteenth century sums up the castle's magnificent park and gardens: 'If Versailles did not exist, Beloeil would be the most beautiful garden in Europe'.

The first sight of Mons as you approach the city is of its Baroque belfry described by Victor Hugo as 'an enormous coffee pot, flanked below the belly level by four medium-sized teapots'. It is referred to locally as 'the castle' because it is cheek-by-jowl with the remains of one which used to crown the hill belonging to the Counts of Hainaut. You can still visit the old underground passages and the chapel of Saint Caliste. Mons was famous for bell-casting and the belfry has a carillon of 47. From the summit you get an extensive view. A lift takes you to the top where there is a relief map and explanations in English which give you an idea of the layout of the battlefields.

Like Ypres, Mons has Allied War Cemeteries and there are British and Canadian War Memorials in the town. A bronze plaque on the façade of the Town Hall was placed there as a token of gratitude for food sent by America to Belgium during the First World War. Another American memorial, a granite obelisk some eight miles south of Mons, commemorates the fighting of early September 1944.

The War Museums in the town are crowded with mementoes of the two World Wars including guns presented by the Canadians, drums from famous British regiments and American helmets; photographs and other reminders of the suffering during those dreadful years.

I remember as a child being told the story of the Angels of Mons by an uncle of mine. In August 1914 a fierce battle raged and the enemy in superior numbers forced the British troops to move back. The retreat was skilfully carried out but at a given moment the British halted and faced the oncoming enemy. The explanation offered was that a host of angels in the guise of archers seemed to appear in the sky and this gave courage to the British and apparently proved too much for the Germans who in turn retreated.

The most outstanding building in Mons is the Collegiate Church of Saint Waudru, considered to be one of the most beautiful examples of fifteenth-century Gothic art in Western Europe. It was begun in 1450 by the ladies of Saint Waudru's noble chapter of secular cannonesses. The interior is simple with beautiful fan-shaped arches. It seems somewhat incongruous to see the 'Golden Car' festooned with cavorting cherubs at the back of the church but this is where it remains except on Trinity Sunday.

On this day each year the 'Golden Car' is trundled out and, watched by thousands of people, forms a main feature of the annual procession. Apparently it is associated with a plague which was rife in Mons in 1349. When the religious part of the procession is finished, festivities take over and the battle between Saint George and the Dragon takes place in the Grand Place. Saint George attacks the vast monster with a lance. The dragon's long tail sweeps over the heads of the crowd who cheer on the hero and mock the dragon. A costumed cavalcade of citizens joins in the fun and the tune of a thirteenth-century ballad adds to the noise, being repeated over and over. The festivities continue for three days with street dancing, more parades, concerts and fireworks before Mons returns to its usual calm.

The Town Hall in the Grand Place has a curious little iron statue of a monkey seated on a stone bracket jutting out from the façade. No one can tell you the exact reason why he is there,

but why conjecture when all you have to do to ensure happiness
is to stroke the head of the little animal as you pass!

In 1966 SHAPE – Supreme Headquarters Allied Powers Europe
– moved from Paris to Belgium and its large complex of new
buildings has been set up at Casteau, five miles from Mons where
some 1,800 families are now housed. The Amigo Hotel is close
by at Masnuy Saint Jean. It is part of a small chain based on
the Amigo in Brussels and this one is modern and comfortable
in a lovely wooded setting with a swimming pool and all the
amenities of the present generation of hotels. On a cold winter's
day it is most welcoming to come into the spacious lobby and
have tea or coffee in front of a blazing log fire. It has 60 rooms
and, while staying there, we met the manageress, Mlle Francine
Horckmans and her father. This chance encounter gave an in-
sight into the wood-carving and high-quality furniture industry
which is still today centred on Malines (*Mechelen*) north of Brussels. Owner of one of the oldest and best known 'ateliers' in
Malines, M Horckmans still enjoys practising the craft himself
when he has the time to do it.

In the Middle Ages Belgian wood-carvers were renowned
throughout Europe and their work embellished many a cathedral
and abbey. After a lapse of one and a half centuries, wood-carving regained its popularity and craftsmen from Malines sought
inspiration in the museums of France but sensibly adapted their
products to the dimensions and customs of modern living. Much
of their work found its way to the United States between the
two World Wars. The Wall Street crash and Second World War
acted as a brake on progress but it is now poised to take advan-
tage of the explosion in the popularity of wooden furniture cur-
rently led by the Scandinavians.

Another most unusual and delightful haven for travellers is at
Roisin about 20 miles south west of Mons, close to French border
– the Auberge du Caillou-qui-bique. Not only is good food served
in the ambience of a private house but it was once owned by the
celebrated Belgian poet Emile Verhaeren who wrote much of
his work here. There is a little museum in the garden and you

can experience a 15-minute slide show which is artistically presented with a taped commentary in various languages.

If you drive down the Charleroi road from Mons and pass
Saint Symphorien you come to the small town of Binche. Its
annual carnival takes place every Shrove Tuesday and the procession and dance of the 'Gilles' is the great feature here. Boys
and men wear very exotic and expensive gold, white, black and
red padded suits which are decorated with lion motifs and hung
around the waist with gilded bells. Their hats are like white top-
pers edged with long white or coloured ostrich plumes. They
carry baskets of oranges which they shower over the crowds with
gay abandon. Truckloads of the fruit have arrived before the
great day so that the baskets can be easily replenished. Shop-
keepers and householders along the route cover their windows
with chicken wire to avoid damage – even the stands before the
Town Hall are protected by high wire screens.

The 'Gilles' gather together and, doing a shuffling tango-like
dance, make their way towards the Grand Place which is cleared
before their arrival by mounted police. Perhaps a thousand
'Gilles', ostrich plumes waving in semi-circles as they tango forward, gradually congregate in the square continuing to dance
to the catchy 'Gille' tune. All the time they pelt oranges into the
watching crowd. Those young men who are not dressed in 'Gille'
uniform carry inflated sheep bladders, which look like odd-shaped
balloons and with these they whack onlookers.

The carnival is a fascinating spectacle and draws large crowds
of visitors but it is only fair to warn that a blow from a sheep
bladder can sting and that the oranges are not lobbed but hurled
so that many burst. Leave your spectacles off and do not wear
clothes which cannot be washed. Orange skins are almost as
effective as banana skins for upsetting mother-in-law! No wonder
our word 'binge' comes from Binche!

6. Bruges and West Flanders

Are you looking for a quaint medieval town with tiny houses turning gabled walls towards narrow streets and trees reflected in canals with diminutive bridges? If you are, and would also enjoy lush parkland, picturesque squares, grassy ramparts, fanciful guild and almshouses; Lilliputian beguinage buildings overshadowed by trees which Winston Churchill loved to paint, or perhaps even an up-to-date Holiday Inn with gabled façade in harmony with the rest of the town – then Bruges is the place for you.

Its fifteenth-century golden ambience still remains. From the twelfth to the sixteenth century the town was the largest commercial city in the north of Europe, a centre for the English and Scandinavian trade as well as the emporium of Hanseatic, Venetian and other Italian merchants. At the height of its medieval prosperity it had a population of 200,000. Among its treasures you can visit its Gothic Town Hall, town chancellery and its famous belfry, 353 feet high, built between the thirteenth and fifteenth centuries. Its melodious carillon was installed in 1743.

When Flanders revolted against Maximilian of Austria it was a great blow to the town. Insecurity and the silting up of the Zwin caused rich merchants to move to Antwerp. Later, from 1794 until 1814, when Flanders was annexed to France, many historic buildings were plundered or demolished. The twentieth century saw a revival with the new access to the sea due to the creation of Zeebrugge harbour and the Baudouin Canal.

Through good times and bad Bruges has retained its charm. Much of its artistic heritage is in the form of gabled palatial houses and its art treasures have been bequeathed by such famous bodies as the Flemish school of painting with its unequalled masterpieces by Memling, Van Eyck, Hugo Van der Goes, Gerard David and other famous artists.

The centre of Bruges is so delightful with its narrow streets, beguinage, Saint John's Hospital and Memling Museum, churches and small buildings that the only way to see and enjoy it all is to walk. Most places are within a few minutes of each other so that the visitor will not tire quickly.

The Tourist Office in the Market Square will help with guides, maps or advice and being in the heart of the city this is a good starting place for sightseeing. The square is impressive, covering over two acres and if you are lucky you may be able to park your car. In the centre there are statues of Jan Breidel and Pieter de Coninck, heroes of the Battle of the Golden Spurs in 1302. The belfry, immortalized for American visitors in a poem by Longfellow, is flanked by two side wings of the vast market and the main Post Office is to the left of the Government Palace. I had heard many references made to Longfellow's poem, *The Belfry of Bruges,* when reading of the city but have never seen one line of it quoted so I had to find out what Longfellow thought all those years ago. The poem is too long to include in full but here are a few lines which might well describe the market square and the memories it evokes today. The poet, having climbed to the top of the belfry in the early morning, describes the city at his feet and continues :

> *Not a sound rose from the city at that early morning hour*
> *But I heard a heart of iron beating in the ancient tower*
>
> *From their nests beneath the rafters sang the swallows*
>   *wild and high,*
> *And the world, beneath me sleeping, seemed more distant*
>   *than the sky.*

Then most musical and solemn, bringing back the
    olden times,
With their strange unearthly changes rang the
    melancholy chimes

Like the psalms from some old cloister, when the nuns
    sing in the choir;
And the great bell tolled among them, like the chanting
    of a friar.

Visions of the days departed, shadowy phantoms filled
    my brain;
They who lived in history only seemed to walk the
    earth again.

All the Foresters of Flanders – mighty Baldwin Bras de Fer,
Lyderick du Bucq and Cressy, Philip, Guy de Dampierre.

I beheld the pageants splendid, that adorned these days
    of old
Stately dames, like Queens attended knights who bore
    the Fleece of Gold.

Lombard and Venetian merchants with deep laden argosies;
Ministers from twenty nations; more than royal pomp
    and ease.

I beheld proud Maximilian, kneeling humbly on
    the ground;
I beheld the gentle Mary hunting her hawk and hound.

I beheld the Flemish weavers, with Namur and Julien bold
Marching homeward from the bloody battle of the
    spurs of gold.

Saw the fight at Minnewater, saw the White Hoods
    moving West,
Saw great Artevelde victorious scale the Golden Dragon's
    nest

Then the sound of drums aroused me. The awakened
    city's roar
Chased the phantoms I had summoned back into their
    graves once more

Hours had passed away like minutes; and before I
    was aware,
Lo! the shadow of the belfry cross the sun illumined square.

If you leave the square along the Breidelstraat you come almost immediately to the 'Burg' – another medieval square. It was built by Baldwin I, first Duke of Flanders, in 870 and consisted of a castle, a chapel, a prison and hostage house. It was protected by wide moats and walls with three gates. Parts of these buildings have been restored or replaced by others but you can get an idea of the original outline. Here is the famous Basilica of the Holy Blood, the beautiful Gothic Town Hall, the sixteenth-century Old Recorders House, the Provost's House and the Court of Justice.

The relic of the Holy Blood was presented to Dierick of Alsace, Count of Flanders in 1150, by the Patriarch of Jerusalem in recognition of bravery during the Second Crusade. It was brought to Flanders by the Count's chaplain who had it tied about his neck. The small crystal phial with a golden stopper hung with silver chains, is said to contain a portion of the blood-stained water washed from the body of Christ by Joseph of Arimathea. This tiny phial has been through several vicissitudes. During the fourteenth century it was thrown into the river when people from Ghent invaded the town. Three days later it was seen gleaming in the water by sisters in the beguinage and rescued.

When Calvinism stalked the city 200 years later the sacred relic was concealed in the house of a burgher of Spanish descent and during the French Revolution and the Napoleonic wars it was hidden in the garrets and cellars by people of trust until it was returned to its rightful place in the Chapel of the Holy

Blood, where it has remained in safe keeping ever since. It is put on display each Friday during the morning and from 3.00 to 3.30 in the afternoon.

Crowds of visitors and local people throng the streets of Bruges when it is borne triumphantly in procession in a magnificent golden reliquary on Ascension Day. This pageant is one of the most important religious processions during the year in Northern Europe. Hundreds of citizens take part, dressed to represent Biblical figures.

The procession starts after lunch following high mass in the cathedral. There is a military band and banners and flags are carried. The procession itself is led by young girls in blue mantles singing the *'Veni Creator'*. Tableaux of Biblical scenes follow one after the other but the highlight of the festival is the appearance of the golden shrine containing the phial of Holy Blood. This is borne aloft by bishops and clergy, followed by members of religious orders, magistrates and the Confraternity of the Holy Blood in picturesque medieval costumes. Housefronts are decorated, candles glimmer on window sills, church bells toll and the procession takes about an hour to pass. It is a holy, solemn yet joyous occasion.

The building which houses the phial of Holy Blood during the rest of the year, although called the basilica, is joined to the Town Hall and consists of two oratories, one superimposed on the other, the Chapel of Saint Basil at ground level and the Chapel of the Holy Blood above. You reach the latter by a staircase. Gothic in style, its stained-glass windows show portraits of several Counts of Flanders. The pulpit is in the form of a world globe carved from a single piece of oak by Pulinx. By a simple, white marble altar there is a plaque which reads:

The relic of the Holy Blood is found behind the tabernacle of this altar. According to tradition the relic was brought to Bruges by Derrick of Alsace, Count of Flanders 1128-1168, founder of this chapel of Saint Basil and the Holy Blood. The rock crystal phial which contains the coagulated blood is preserved in a glass cylinder with golden crowns and this has remained intact since the arrival in Bruges as testified by historical data from as far back as 1250. The city of Bruges is intimately connected with the present relic and has had it in safe keeping without interruption during past centuries. It has been venerated and through it the person of Our Lord. That is why people come here just not to see the relic but also to pray.

The tiny room used as a small museum just to one side of the chapel has some paintings and a few antiquities but most interesting are the two reliquaries which are used to encase the Holy Blood. The one generally in use is of silver and was given by Archduke Albert and Archduchess Isabella in 1611. The second and more beautiful is of gold and gilt studded with gems and alongside it a plaque reads :

This piece of art of gold and silver ornamented with precious stones is made by Jan Crabbe, goldsmith of Bruges, 1617. His coat of arms and those of the members of the noble fraternity of the Holy Blood adorn the base. The crown suspended above the golden box belonged to Mary of Burgundy who died 1482. This box is empty. In it is placed the relic on the day of the annual procession. Every Friday and daily also from 3-17 May the relic is exposed in the basilica. The relic is kept behind the white marble altar on the right-hand side of the church.

Although Gothic architecture throughout Belgium is superb, Bruges' Town Hall, housing the two oratories at one side, is one of the most splendid examples. Its main hall has a groined ceiling with wooden pendants hanging from the vaulting like delicately formed stalactites. The present wall decorations show events of historic importance and were painted by two Flemish artists Albert and Juliaan De Vriendt, between 1895 and 1905. There are nine scenes :

1   Triumphal return of the Bruges warriors from the Battle of the Golden Spurs at Kortrijk.

2 Foundation of the Order of the Golden Fleece, by Philip the Good, Duke of Burgundy in 1430.

3 Derrick of Alsace, Count of Flanders, brings the Relic of the Holy Blood to the Church of Saint Basil in 1150.

4 The refectory of Saint John's Hospital.

5 The Bruges municipality renews the privileges of the Teutonic Hanseatic League.

6 Philip of Alsace, Count of Flanders, grants a charter to Bruges in 1190.

7 The Bruges magistrate visits the studio of Jan Van Eyck in 1433.

8 Jan Britto, a Bruges printer, sells his books in Bruges in 1446.

9 Lodewijk van Male, Count of Flanders, lays the foundation stone of the Town Hall in 1376.

One of the windows near the western door has a balcony with slender, graceful railings which was used as a pulpit during Holy week while crowds below listened to sermons and joined together in prayer. From the same balcony the counts of Flanders received the fealty of their subjects who also swore to defend the honour of Bruges.

If you walk beneath the arch between the Town Hall and the Recorder's House – a lovely Renaissance building whose façade is topped with three statues representing Justice flanked by Moses on the left and Aaron on the right – you come to the Tanners' Guild Hall, now an exhibition centre. You go along the Rozenhoedkaai, where swans glide along the canal disturbing the reflections of shady trees and stepped gables.

You are now close to the city's picture gallery, the Groeninge Museum, built in 1930 over the site of a former abbey. The only word to describe this small, air-conditioned building with its low ceilings is 'charming'. You walk through a gateway into a small garden before going into its octagonal entrance hall. There are only a few paintings in each of the 15 rooms so that the separate masterpieces can be enjoyed to the full. They are hung at eye level and the lighting is excellent. Here you will see some of the most beautiful examples of the famous Bruges school of painting. Jan Van Eyck's portrait of his wife shows a hair style so outré that it would puzzle any modern hairdresser. His painting of Canon van der Paelen, represented kneeling before the Virgin under the patronage of Saint George, is so faultlessly detailed that, through the pince nez which the Canon holds over a page of the Bible, you can read the magnified words. When Van Eyck settled in Bruges his wife bore him a son and Philip the Good, a great admirer of the artist, was sponsor at the christening.

Other Flemish artists featured include Van der Goes, Van der Weyden, and Memling. Gerard David, born at Oudewater in Holland, was the last great master of the Bruges school and in this museum you will see his most extraordinary painting of a man being skinned alive; a horrifying subject so unlike his usual work that the reason for it is worth recounting. 'The Slaying of Sisamnes' was commissioned during the local burghers vehement quarrelling with Maximilian. It was intended to hang in the Court of Justice and perhaps could be taken as a warning for disloyalty. Gerard David married the daughter of the dean of the local Goldsmiths' Guild and through his painting became one of Bruges' leading citizens. He died in 1523 and was buried in the Church of Our Lady.

The Church of Our Lady, with its imposing 375-feet high brick tower, visible from most points in the centre of Bruges, also houses paintings from the Bruges school including David's 'The Transfiguration'. Two Burgundian tombs contain the remains of Charles the Bold and his daughter Maria who was killed in a hunting accident. In a black marble niche on the altar in the southern nave stands an exceptionally lovely treasure of the church – an exquisite Virgin and Child by Michelangelo.

Across the Mariastraat from the church there is the entrance of St John's Hospital. Founded in 1188 it is an unspoilt architectural example of that period. It is also exceptional in that, although it is still used as a hospital, it contains the Memling

14 Zimmer tower in Lier

Museum and possibly one of the oldest pharmacies in the world – certainly the most interesting.

A tale is told that Memling was wounded at Nancy and was sheltered and cured at the hospital. To show his gratitude he is said to have painted for the Hospitallers of Saint John and these pictures have been added to down through the years so that today the collection is unique. The most outstanding work of his later years depicts the story of Saint Ursula in six intricate miniature scenes. These tiny, crowded paintings line the sides of a shrine containing a relic of the saint. The variety of landscapes and delicacy of the many minute figures denote hours of skill and patience. The Memling collection is displayed in a thirteenth-century hospital ward. Paintings hang on the stone walls and in the centre is the focal point – the reliquary of Saint Ursula.

Before you leave the grounds of Saint John's Hospital you must visit the medieval pharmacy on the opposite side of the entrance. A door opens on to cloisters where some antique furniture is on display. If you turn sharp right you will come to the door which is the entrance to the pharmacy. As soon as you have crossed the threshold you feel you have stepped back into the Middle Ages. Here are all sizes of old-fashioned apothecary's scales, silver pestles and mortars, one so large that if the pestle is struck gently on the side of the mortar it chimes like a church bell. Great elbow-high wooden counters have masses of tiny drawers, each with its own label, which slide in and out as smoothly as the day they were made. There are rows of lovely old china jars which used to contain herbs and drugs. A special cupboard hangs on the wall with an enormous key still in place. Inside it is again fitted with tiny drawers. The door has a word of warning on the outside, 'Poisons'. Most interesting of all is the fact that this old-world but beautifully equipped pharmacy was used until recently.

Many visitors think that the most picturesque place in Bruges is the beguinage with its tranquil surroundings. You enter the wooded, parklike grounds over a humpback bridge. Going

15 Château Beloeil

through a quaint gateway you discover a row of tiny, white cottages edged with low walls and minute flower beds overlooking a lawn as green as a village cricket pitch. The overhanging branches of lofty old trees fleck the green with shadows on sunny days. Today the beguines have been replaced by nuns who still wear the black robes and white linen head-dress painted by Memling.

Originally beguines were either the widows of knights killed in the Crusades or unmarried sisters or daughters of such families. They did not wish to become nuns, in that they shut themselves up in convents for the rest of their lives, but they did wish to spend their time doing good works and tending the sick. In a sense a beguinage was a type of 'open' yet 'closed' community where women were free to come and go but desired to devote themselves to godly and charitable pursuits. If they wished to marry or return to their families they were free to do so.

You can leave the beguinage by walking over an aged stone bridge across the Minnewater – Lake of Love. One wonders if this romantic stretch of water inspired Longfellow when he visited Bruges as a young man, to call his Indian maiden in 'Hiawatha', his best known poem, *Minnehaha* – Laughing Water. The Minnewater reflects a row of trees, which are illuminated at night, and also the arched bridge, a sluice house, the usual lovely stepped gables and the tower of the Church of Our Lady. Swans curve through the placid water, as white as the reflected clouds, and now and then glide towards the grassy banks to wait under weeping willow branches, hoping for tasty pieces of bread from passers by.

There are several other museums and places to visit within a few minutes' walk and still in the centre of Bruges. Next to the Groeninge museum there is a small one for old carriages and sleighs. Another adjoining one is the Brangwyn which was given to Bruges by the British artist Frank Brangwyn. It has some 300 works by the artist which include oil paintings, etchings, drawings and watercolours. Near the Church of Our Lady is the Gruut-house Palace, a museum with a wealth of carved oak and huge fireplaces in its great rooms; it also has various collections, two being of ceramics and priceless lace.

As you walk through Bruges each corner reveals a quay, a statue or perhaps a secluded bench overlooking a stretch of water. If you are not fond of walking a most pleasant way to see Bruges is by water. Tourist boats wend their leisurely way around the canals, which have been cleaned in recent years so that no unwelcome smell reaches you as you round a bend, which unfortunately one cannot say about Ghent, or even Venice!

Still in Bruges and not far from the centre of the city there are other unexpected things to see – such as the Bruges' bear. At the corner of Academiestraat, about 15 feet up on the side of a building in a niche there is the statue of a white bear – the 'Beertje van de Loget' known, like the Mannekin Pis in Brussels, as the 'oldest inhabitant of the city'.

The niche is on the side of the Poortersloge building, not far from 'Ter Buerze', where the first exchange transactions were held in Bruges. The Poortersloge was formerly used as a meeting place of the local burghers and 'White Bear Guild'. The animal stands on his hind paws and holds the shield of Bruges in his front paws. He is dressed in different uniforms and robes on certain occasions. The last time I saw him he was wearing a red military coat. Undressed or otherwise he is a most charming beast.

The Jerusalem Church, founded in 1427, is an odd mixture of Oriental and Gothic architecture and was built by the Adornes family from Genoa. It is still privately owned but arrangements can be made with the nuns for access by appointment. The original intention was to make an exact copy of the Church of the Holy Sepulchre in Jerusalem and, to this end, three journeys were made to the Holy City. However it was destroyed by fire soon after it was erected and the present building is best described as a close approximation. Stairways lead to the upper Chapel of the Holy Cross as indeed they do in Jerusalem. In the crypt there is a model of the Holy Sepulchre Church in Jerusalem and

a gilded reliquary of the fifteenth century. The armorial bearings of the Adornes family decorate the church and members of
the family are depicted in the fifteenth-century stained-glass
windows.

In a little street running down one side of the church there is
a lacemaking school and a folklore museum. The latter has been
converted from eight adjoining tiny cottages connected together
as a string of rooms, each featuring different things. The lacemaking school teaches children and is open to tourists.

The College of Europe in Bruges was the first university
centre for European studies to be created after the Second World
War and was opened in 1949. It does not depend on any national
authority and is under the guidance of an administrative council
which includes representatives of European governments, insti-
tutions and bodies that give the College financial support. The
students must have a thorough knowledge of French and English,
be single and less than 30 years of age. Their number is limited
to 60 each academic year, and they are chosen by selection
boards which sit in 13 European countries. Those from countries
where there is no such board or who wish to follow courses at
their own expense can apply directly to the college which, in
certain cases, can make grants towards their costs. The Bruges
Holiday Inn Hotel normally accommodates about 28 students
attending courses.

Bruges has many hotels but the Holiday Inn is an outstanding
one. It is situated within walking distance of the centre of the
town a few minutes from the main station, and has 131 air-conditioned rooms. It has an indoor heated swimming pool, sauna
and a very good restaurant and coffee shop. Yet what really
makes it different is that it has been built over the site of an
old Capucine convent and has incorporated some of the old
building. The façade was removed during the construction and
was then restored so that it fits in with the other typical gabled
buildings close to it. The original chapel has been restored at the
back of the hotel and can be used by the public. It is non-denomi-
national and a very popular place for weddings. Indeed if the

reception is held at the Holiday Inn the guests do not even need to leave the building!

The bar is fitted with some of the convent furniture and the Assistant Inn Keeper, Ben Ancher, told me that two aged nuns had visited him and asked to see over their erstwhile convent. One wished to visit her old room and was mildly outraged when she discovered that the site of her celibate years now formed part of the bar!

In Bruges and its surrounding areas there are facilities for a wide variety of sport and recreational activities, including golf, sailing, swimming, skiing and skating but history beckons everywhere. About three miles from the crowded city of Bruges is the quiet little town of Damme which can be reached by a picturesque old canal or the road alongside it. Either way is attractive for the waterway is lined with shady trees and green meadows. There is little traffic and an atmosphere of languor increases as you reach the town. Not many coaches disgorge tourists in the main square and there are few taxis or motor vehicles of any kind. It is a joy to park your car in the large empty town square.

Damme, once Bruges' crowded port, could accommodate some 100 ships bringing merchandise from all parts of the western world. But that was six and more centuries ago. In those days, as the name implies, they had to build banks to dam the waters and the Zwin gave access from the North Sea. The great naval battle of Sluis, in which Edward III destroyed the French fleet and secured the command of the channel, was fought in the year 1340 at the mouth of the Zwin. About 1395 this channel began to show signs of silting up and during the next century the process proved rapid. A treaty was signed at Damme between Maximilian and the people of Bruges in 1490 and later the channel completely closed up and the port was no more. Yet because Damme became a quiet village and warring armies left it alone, it has some remarkable old buildings which are well preserved. In the spacious square facing you, with its double stairway guarded by two dignified stone lions holding shields, is the Gothic Town Hall. Inside there is a museum and the open tower has two of the oldest bells in Flanders which were cast in 1392 and 1398.

The tower of the brick church of Our Lady, dating from 1180, is a landmark across the dunes and the church behind it, although a ruin, was the first example of a Flemish 'hall church'. A fifteenth-century gabled house, to the right of the enchanting Town Hall, is now the Jacob van Maerlant Museum. It was here that Charles the Bold and Margaret of York, sister of Edward IV were married on 2 July 1468.

On the subject of peace and serenity, the many cemeteries of Ypres, 638 of them in the town and environs, have the same tranquil atmosphere. Relatives, tourists and friends visit the well-tended graves for this is the 'Holy Ground of British Arms'. Throughout the long four years of the First World War Ypres was occupied by British troops. It was never more than seven miles, sometimes less than three, from the front line. The heroism of the inhabitants themselves was unwavering. Even when the Burgomaster and three eminent citizens were taken as hostages, when the first deadly gas clouds shrouded the town and day by day buildings turned into mounds of burning debris, they did not flinch. A shell tore off the roof of St Peter's Church one Sunday morning but the service continued. The wounded had to be tended in what was left of the cellars but still the town held.

So many names bring back grim memories of those who fought there: 'Hooge' where furious fighting took place; a junction on the road from Zillebeke known as 'Hell Fire Corner'; 'Sanctuary Wood' and 'Mount Sorel' forever linked with the Canadians. It was near the latter that the line was carried by the Germans for nearly a mile. The Canadians retook the trenches a few days later. Ypres was in the forefront of a salient and thousands and thousands of British soldiers were killed in its defence – so many that thousands of them have no known graves. What Verdun was to the French, Ypres was to the British. The devastation was such that at one time it was doubtful if the town could ever be rebuilt. Yet like the phoenix it was to rise again and in 1920 received the British Military Cross and the French Croix de Guerre. Ypres became a place of pilgrimage and those soldiers who had lived through the town's anguish were never to forget 'Wipers' as Tommy Atkins called it.

As a suitable place to build a lasting memorial to the 250,000 officers and men who lost their lives at Ypres, the site of the Old Menin Gate on the city ramparts at the eastern entrance to the town was chosen. A new Menin Gate, a magnificent arch with a couchant lion on the summit looking eastward towards Germany, was erected. This classical structure was designed by the late Sir Reginald Blomfield, RA and engraved on the walls are the names of 54,896 soldiers who have no known grave (the remaining 34,957 names of the missing are inscribed on panels at Tyne Cot Cemetery on the Passchendaele ridge about six miles east of Ypres).

The memorial was completed in 1927 and, in the presence of His Majesty King Albert 1 of the Belgians, was unveiled by Field Marshal Viscount Plumer, who had commanded the British Second Army which was responsible for the defence of Ypres during the greater part of the war.

A very short time after the unveiling took place a group of citizens conceived the idea that it would be a grateful gesture on the part of the townspeople if they could pay a nightly tribute to the memory of those who had fallen in the defence of the town. So the ceremony of sounding the 'Last Post' at the Menin Gate every evening came into being. At nine o'clock in the summer and eight o'clock during the winter, two Belgian buglers take up their position on the road beneath the archway. The police hold up the traffic and, as the hour strikes from the cathedral tower, the melancholy notes of the 'Last Post' carry over the ramparts.

On Armistice Day in November 1968, the 50th anniversary of the First World War, there was a television link-up between Ypres and London. BBC crews had spent the previous few days in Belgium in preparation with Roland Annoot, who was in charge of the local arrangements. When the day arrived the sun shone brightly in London but in Ypres the weather was uncertain. Roland became more and more anxious as the time for the broadcast approached because a mist arose swirling about the cemeteries. However the cameras recorded the scene live as there was no local alternative, and he returnd to his office convinced that the telecast must have been a failure. To his surprise and delight congratulations poured in from both countries and the BBC sent a small shield in recognition of the occasion. Far from marring the occasion the mist had created just the right atmosphere.

Today Ypres is a modern thriving town but the main square, the second largest in Belgium, has been rebuilt just as it was centuries ago, so that the old rubs shoulders with the new. Time has dimmed the horror of those momentous four years 1914 to 1918. 'Hell Fire Corner' has a small stone memorial to show where the Germans were halted. 'Sanctuary Wood' has a lovely Canadian maple tree avenue leading to it. 'Hooge Crater' cemetery is peaceful with its flowers and green grass between the small white headstones. Cemeteries are everywhere and their simplicity is touching. They are mostly rectangular in shape with a stone of remembrance at one side, an altar-shaped plaque with the engraved words from Ecclesiasticus, 'Their name liveth for evermore'. A tall crucifix guards rows of graves, each of which has a white marble headstone with the name, regiment and date of death of its occupant. Flowers bloom before many of these and the rest is smooth green lawn. The largest is Tyne Cot which contains 11,847 graves and three German pill boxes now ivy covered. Queen Elizabeth II saw it during her visit in 1968. One French cemetery has a mound of stones brought from Picardy. The German cemeteries have grey headstones placed flat on the ground.

Ypres had a most important linen and lace trade and its thirteenth-century Gothic Cloth Hall, in the main square with a façade over 150 yards in length, was renowned for its splendour and beauty – the same as its replica has today. A similar building enterprise was carried out for the shelled cathedral which was rebuilt over its own foundations. You can still see the tomb of Bishop Jansen whose studies of St Augustine caused much controversy during the seventeenth century. As well as these two important buildings the square has many reconstructed seventeenth-century house façades and there are several excellent restaurants. A safari park is on the outskirts of town and the annual 'Procession of the Cats' is a lively and spectacular occasion with true carnival atmosphere.

Cats were required in great numbers during the middle ages to deal with the mice rampant in the Cloth Hall. When the great yearly sales were over and the storage space empty the mice vanished and the cats themselves then became the problem. It is said that in order to get rid of them the inhabitants conceived the effective, if barbarous, practice of hurling them from the belfry to the ground. Since 1938 this idea has been revived, the great difference being that the cats today are toy ones. Hundreds of spectators crowd around the foot of the belfry in the hope of catching one of the souvenir toys. Cat worship has always been linked with witches so toy witches are also thrown by the carnival jester. This is all part of the magnificent procession held late in the evening which has floats devoted to the history of the town and, of course, the cats.

It is often said, perhaps ironically, that the harder one works the more spare time one has! Unquestionably proper allocation of time to different activities and careful programming is of the essence and no two people work in exactly the same way. A Deputy Burgomaster of Ypres, Gerard Sercu, is a case in point. He has his own business and runs a workshop for the handicapped, designs ornaments for the church and takes his public duties seriously. I asked him how he ran his day.

Gerard Sercu, although he left school at the age of 14, speaks 5 languages. He gets up at 7.30 each morning, drinks a glass of milk and then goes to the workshop. The people there are paid normal wages and his enthusiasm carries them along for he believes that this factory can put in the same work during the day as more orthodox places and their output measures up to his expectations. He gets home by 10 o'clock and reads his mail after which he goes straight to the Town Hall. Back again for a 1 o'clock lunch with his wife Nina, he leaves his house at 2 o'clock to go to his business. By 5 o'clock he is back in the Town Hall where there will be meetings, reunions, receptions and often a banquet later at night. Every Sunday there is a reception in the morning at the Town Hall and perhaps people to meet there in the afternoon. Gerard Sercu says he has no hobbies because he regards all that he does as his hobbies! He is a lawyer by profession but has been on Ypres council for 25 years. As with most legal men he tells a good story.

During one of the battles of Ypres in the First World War a fleet of double-decker London buses was used to rush troops to the front. One of these has been a treasured possession of the town ever since. It was christened 'Old Bill' after the famous Bruce Bairnsfather cartoon. Perhaps the best known of these drawings was of immortal soldier Old Bill looking dazed and seated in a deep shell hole. On being asked what he was doing there he replied: 'If you can find a better 'ole – go to it!'

Two or three years ago London Transport offered the municipality a modern London bus if they cared to come and collect it. Gerard Sercu volunteered and, although he had never driven such a large vehicle before, he got it to Dover without any trouble. There its height prevented it from getting aboard the Dover-Ostend ferry and only the Dover-Dunkerque one could accommodate it. On arrival the French had a number of excellent reasons why it could not be allowed to land but they did not know Gerard. In the end he made a triumphal progress to his home town but he says he will let someone else collect the next bus!

Some 24 miles from Bruges and, like Ypres close to the French frontier, lies Kortrijk (Courtrai). It ranks, after Brussels and Antwerp, as Belgium's third most important industrial town, and is crossed by the European motorway linking Paris and the north of France to Ghent, Antwerp and Hamburg. It is a great shopping centre and the French, who come across the border particularly on Saturdays, call it 'Petit Paris'.

Kortrijk has always had a commercial background for which the river Lys which winds through it – its 'Golden River' – is largely responsible. In the sixteenth century Kortrijk became a centre of the flax industry at the time when linen began to rival wool for the manufacture of cloth. The water of the Lys was found to have special qualities for the process of 'retting' flax – softening and separating the fibres – and Kortrijk's damascs were much in demand during the next two centuries both by European Courts and anyone else who could afford them.

Kortrijk is still a leader in the production of cloth, since it has proved adaptable and now makes fabrics based on man-made fibres as well as fine linens and cottons.

Whole sections of the town were razed during the last World War but two old towers remain. The Tours du Broel are part of the old fortifications flanking one of the Lys bridges, and one has been converted into an interesting little museum.

Kortrijk seems to have been noteworthy also for its medical background. During the eighteenth century the local beguinage acted as a hospital for wounded soldiers for several years. In recent times the town has housed part of Leuven University where Arts, Sciences and Medicine are studied and there is an Institute for Nursing Science. Its seven hospitals are well known and near its Archaeological Museum there is a statue of one of its native sons, Jean Palfijn, a surgeon who died in 1730 and who invented forceps. To the right of the belfry in the Town Square there is another statue, this time of de Haerne, a famous benefactor of the deaf and dumb.

The seventeenth-century beguinage has a small chapel, the Chapel of Our-Lady-in-the-Snow, where the pious come to pray to be cured of all kinds of mental illness. Prayers are also offered to other saints for protection from specific disabilities; Saint Apollonia – toothache; Saint Godeliva – eye trouble and sore throats; Saint Margaret of Antioch – cramps and labour; and

Saint Francis of the Seven Wounds who protects from cancer, sore throats and nervous diseases.

It has been mentioned before that beguinages probably originated to house the surplus of marriageable girls and widows caused by wars, feuds and the crusades. Although Belgium had by far the largest number, some 94 at one time, in the Middle Ages they were not exclusive to that country. Germany had 54, the Netherlands 38, France 36, Austria-Hungary 3, Switzerland and Italy 2 each and England and Poland 1 each. Perhaps a reflection on the male attrition rate!

The Kortrijk beguinage has been damaged and restored many times. Its 42 Baroque houses with narrow cobbled streets are edged by two churches. Its entrance gateway is a few yards to the south of Saint Martin's Church and it is confined to the north by the Church of Our Lady.

Kortrijk's great historic victory was the Battle of the Golden Spurs in 1302. It was the first time that armoured knights were defeated by ordinary foot soldiers and was to create the foundations of a future independent Belgium. The Flemish Guilds, determined to break the French yoke, fielded an army of 8,000 to 10,000 men; some 900 archers and the rest foot soldiers with clubs and pikes. The battle took place on Groeninge Field near the river Lys. The French attacked first but found themselves against a tough wall of pikes and clubs which would not give way. The battle was a short one of about three hours. During that time over 1,000 French noblemen and some 70 Counts and Barons were annihilated and 700 pairs of golden spurs were collected from the corpses. These glittering trophies were hung in the Church of Our Lady.

The Church of Our Lady is the oldest in Kortrijk, going back to the thirteenth century. The Golden Spurs have long since gone but it has one special treasure without equal – Van Dyck's masterpiece 'The Raising of the Cross'.

The present Town Hall, a mixture of late Gothic and Renaissance styles, was built in 1519. Statues of the Counts of Flanders range along the façade. The building was renovated in 1962 and

has some splendid modern rooms but happily the chamber of the
Aldermen and Councillors, used as a wedding room and reception hall, has remained intact. The graceful Gothic mantelpiece
is undoubtedly the showpiece with lace-fine carvings. It was
completed in 1527. The wooden figures at the top represent the
virtues of devotion, humility, generosity, chastity, love of one's
fellow creatures, meekness and vigilance. In the central panel the
contrary vices are shown: idolatry, pride, avarice, envy,
gluttony, anger and indolence. In the lowest panel the vices are
represented in eight scenes. In one of the top panels a man is seen
defying everything in order to reach a woman locked up in a
tower surrounded by a moat.

Examples of polychrome sculptural art on rafter bases against
the ceiling show the fatal influence of woman on man in several
erotic vignettes. The Greek philosopher Aristotle is on all fours
with bit and bridle held in his teeth. The Indian woman Cam-
paspe has mounted this unusual horse and is holding reins in her
left hand while the other grips a whip raised to strike him. Sar-
danapal, the Assyrian, is shown enslaved by women of his Court,
so much so that he is helping them with their spinning. King
Solomon is being persuaded by women to sacrifice to idols. Eve,
of course, is tempting Adam to eat an apple. On one rafter support there is a mask with a padlocked mouth and another has
two heads kissing.

The whole of the Belgian coast is within the same province of
West Flanders as Kortrijk. Sometimes called Maritime Flanders
it is the province nearest to the British Isles and there are relics
of the Roman occupation in Kortrijk before the invasion of
England about 43 BC.

Knokke-Heist comprises some five townships at the north-
western end of the coast nearest the Dutch border – Heist, Duinbergen, Albertstrand, Knokke and Zoute. If you enter Belgium
from Zeebrugge, Heist is the first place you come to with a small
fishing port and it acts as a dormitory area for local tradespeople
and factory workers. Duinbergen is a small garden city. At
Albertstrand you will find the casino which offers cinema and

theatre performances with international artists as well as the usual gambling and nightclub facilities. Behind it is the luxurious La Reserve Hotel which is under the same management as the casino. This enables four clubs to be at the disposal of guests and gala evenings with international cabarets are frequently presented in the season. Crimson and blue suites offer the unusual facility of wall safes, presumably for your winnings, and there is a private lake for swimming and boating.

Knokke is the business and administrative centre with shops, offices, banks and supermarkets in the shopping district and numerous hotels, pensions and restaurants.

Zoute, nearest the Dutch border has charming villas, woods and gardens and is a delightful residential area. The Rustlaan is the main fashionable shopping street. The former summer residence of King Leopold III is in the Zwin, a 300-acre nature reserve of which part lies in Holland. It is often flooded and has bird and plant life unique in Belgium. The residence itself is now a famous restaurant, the Chalet du Zwin.

Ostend, which became known as the 'Queen of the Belgian Beaches' between the two Great Wars, has over 200 hotels and the Wellington race-course. It is flanked by several little resorts each with individual appeal. De Haan has its 18-hole golf course and sand yachting is popular at La Panne which is near the French border. Most visitors come to coastal resorts primarily to laze about and enjoy the stretches of golden sand, swimming and sunbathing. Children love it.

7. The Provinces of Namur and Luxembourg

The province of Namur is blessed with many tourist attractions and its capital city, Namur, is well placed for communications. It lies at the confluence of the Sambre and Meuse rivers and has a main rail junction. More recently the coming of the autoroutes has brought renewed importance. The junction of the E40 from the Duchy of Luxembourg to Brussels and the E41 from Northern France to the Ruhr are just to the north of the city.

The rocky promontory in the fork between the two rivers is crowned by a citadel. It is not surprising, due to its strategic position, that the city's history is mostly a military one. It was Don John of Austria's headquarters until he died in 1578. Louis XIV captured it in 1692 followed by William III in 1695. The French recaptured it in 1702. It underwent subsequent sieges and played a prominent part in the defence of Belgium in 1914.

The citadel is now a barracks and the hill on which it stands is a public park of about 200 acres criss-crossed with walks, avenues, and look-outs. The attractive Chateau de Namur on the upper plateau now belongs to the Hotel Amigo chain and has been converted into an hotel so cleverly that there is even a heated swimming pool in the renovated cellars. Further down the slopes is an open-air theatre, forest museum, sports stadium, the renowned Namur hotel school and several beautiful villas. From the citadel the town spreads out below, the point of the junction of the two rivers resembling a gigantic stone ship with a statue of Leopold I acting as a figurehead.

One institution survived from medieval times until recently

when it was discontinued due to the high casualty rate. This was the annual encounter in the Place d'Armes of rival parties mounted on stilts. Galliot, the historian of Namur, says the origin of these jousts is lost in antiquity but considers the use of stilts was due to the frequency with which the town was flooded before the rivers were embanked. A more amusing explanation is that at one time a Duke of Namur became so enraged with pleas from his subjects that he refused to see a delegation whether it came 'on foot, horse, carriage or boat'. A city father thought up the idea that the men should approach the castle on stilts and the Duke was so intrigued that he rewarded their ingenuity by granting their request! Whatever the reason stilts were used in the past they only make their appearance these days at carnival times.

The Meuse is nearly 560 miles long and probably its traffic is only exceeded by that of the Rhine. As with the Rhine its legends are many. In Belgium the stories about the fabulous steed Bayard are part of the lore of the river valley. Bayard was the favourite horse of the four sons of Aymon who fought a long war against Charlemagne. Several castles in the region claim to have sheltered these young men. As for Bayard, he could leap across the Meuse. In Namur there is an ultra-modern statue of him doing this near one of the bridges.

The Baroque Cathedral of Saint Aubain was built in the eighteenth century. The Church of Saint Loup is a century older and has distinctive red marble columns from the quarry at Saint Remy near Rochefort. The town itself is attractive particularly in the old section where eighteenth-century façades are being restored in several narrow streets. Angel Square boasts a flower market beside an enchanting fountain.

At Wepion some three miles to the south you can sample something new in hospitality, the GB Motor Hotel. It is not the conventional motel where you just park your car, get a meal and have a night's sleep but so much more. Certainly there is plenty of space for your car. The 130 large rooms are carefully and well furnished and spread out so that you might almost be alone in your own home. There are naturally several types of room,

16 *Memorial to Lord Uxbridge's leg at Waterloo*

17 *The Bear of Bruges dressed in his military uniform*

18 *The bronze Gille of Binche*

19 *Statue of Renert the Fox in Luxembourg city*

20 *Marc Devos' charming statue of milkmaid, Brussels*

suites, studios with divans and so on, but all have bath, telephone, radio and television. There is a heated swimming pool half inside the hotel and half outside in a charming landscaped garden where, a few yards beyond, the Meuse flows quietly by, over-hung with walnut trees. There are conference rooms, a restaurant and coffee shop, bowling pitch and solarium. For those who like walking, there are paths along the river and in the woods. Perhaps one of the great advantages to the traveller is that part of the sprawling complex has a large supermarket and petrol station so that everything needed is to hand.

It is difficult to know which of the many historic castles in Belgium to visit. Spontin, 15 miles from Namur and 7 from Dinant, is one of the most interesting for it is Belgium's oldest inhabited castle and is open to the public from the beginning of April to the end of September and also every Sunday in the months of March and October. Situated in the attractive valley of the river Bocq whose waters feed its moat, it belongs to Baron Leon de Pierpoint Surmont de Volksberghe. It is not large but has so many unusual points that it is well worth a visit. The draw-bridge can still be operated by its old system of counter weights.

At one time, towards the end of the sixteenth century, it was regarded as a country manor house and, to soften the fortress-like exterior, the towers were corbelled and the windows added.

The interior of the castle is as unusual as the outside. There are secret staircases and a hidden well, the latter was invaluable in times of siege. Panelling is inlaid with pear wood and a section of it hides a watchman's lookout. The library floor is in chess board pattern made up of 4,000 pieces of sandstone set in a mixture of rye meal, lime and mud. A fourteenth-century cup-board conceals the well and coats of mail, swords and cross bows mix with French and Italian furnishings. Each chamber has a different fireplace, the one in the dining room being of irregular stonework of the seventeenth century with a backing of Spanish tiles. The mantelpiece rests on the heads of statues of Adam and Eve at each side in true Acropolis fashion.

When Louis xiv laid siege to Namur he made arrangements

for his morganatic wife, Madame de Maintenon, to live at Dinant, one of the prettiest towns on the Meuse. The older portion is sandwiched between rocky cliffs and the east bank of the river. It is difficult to believe that it has been razed to the ground many times. In 1466, 800 of its citizens were tied back to back and drowned in the river by order of the then Duke of Burgundy. The thirteenth-century church has been restored again and again, its distinctive onion spire which used to house the city's archives, being invariably retrieved from the rubble and repaired. Yet, as with other resilient Belgian towns, Dinant has recovered each time and maintains its gay spirit.

A most relaxing way to visit Dinant from Namur, or *vice versa,* on a sunny summer's day is aboard a slow-moving river boat. You pass steep wooded shores studded with wild flowers and wend your way past tiny green islets. Swans balance on the wash of your ship hoping you will throw them a cheese biscuit while you enjoy a cooling glass of white wine and forget there are such things as jet planes.

Like Namur the town has a cliff-top citadel and another tower-crested hill rising some 400 feet above the river. Montford tower is also referred to as Mont-Fat and there are underground caverns which were uncovered at the turn of the century. Lifts take you to both of these pinnacles to enjoy the view. About a mile south of Dinant there is an unusual rock formation known as Rocher de Bayard. One section of stone has become separated from the main portion to form an obelisk and the road now passes between this and the mother rock. Once again the magic horse, Bayard, comes on the scene. He is said to have kicked the wide cleft in the rock and, having left a great hoof mark behind, bounded in another splendid leap over the river. Napoleon and his army passed through the divide on the way to Waterloo.

If the name of Dinant's main street, Rue Adolphe Sax, strikes a chord it is no mere coincidence for it was this local citizen who invented the saxophone in 1845. The street, always thronged with people, has a casino but more enticing are the shops. Windows are tastefully arranged with brass and copperware for which the district is famous. Dinant *couques* – gingerbread biscuits – are also famous. They are made in moulds so that they turn out like carvings in different shapes and sizes. The variety is amazing. You can eat a *couque* in the form of a church or a folklore character or an animal. Children love choosing animals. I asked one little English girl why she wanted a rabbit to eat. 'I am not going to eat this bunny', she replied indignantly, 'I am going to take him home and use him as an ornament in my bedroom!' The little girl was not far wrong as the biscuits are alleged to keep almost indefinitely.

At Dinant and other Meuse towns you can swim or fish, hire a canoe and shoot small but swiftly flowing rapids, water ski or sail. Golf, tennis and horse riding are there for the asking. For those who like plunging underground to cool grottoes there are many beautiful ones in the Ardennes where ornamental rock formations are skilfully illuminated and you can take a boat along calm subterranean lakes. These reflect such intricately shaped and delicately coloured stalagmites and stalactites that you are suddenly transported into a fantasy world.

If your greatest pleasure is motoring in virtually traffic-free roads the Ardennes is blessed with many twisting ones. Rounding a corner you often come upon a tiny inn where the meals can be simple but delicious. Trout come fresh from one of the many streams and are served *au bleu*. Wild duck and game can be had in the autumn and always through the year there is the famed Ardennes smoked ham, served in paper thin slices and tangy to the taste.

Three miles from Dinant on the uplands above the Meuse you come to the village of Celles. Here, outside the Café Ardennais, you will find one of several German tanks still dotted about the area, reminders of the fierce fighting in the last World War. This one is rather rusty, its gun still pointing towards Dinant, lying literally where it was stopped in its tracks on Christmas Eve 1944. The notice behind the tank reads: 'Here was stopped the von Rundstedt offensive on 24 December 1944'.

On that Christmas Eve Dinant was deserted except for a few

soldiers waiting for the command to blow up the strategic bridge across the Meuse if it was necessary. Some hours before, a German scout car bearing an American star had blown up on a mine at the entrance to Dinant.

At Celles 100 people sheltered uncomfortably in the dark crypt of their ancient church. At the Café Ardennais the owner, small, stout Marthe Monique, was suddenly shaken rigid by an explosion outside. She opened the door and saw several German officers. The lead tank of a long column had just blown up on a mine blocking the road to Dinant. The officers asked her if there were any Americans in the area. She replied that there were many, which was untrue.

For good measure she added : 'Messieurs, the route to Dinant is sown with mines. The Americans were working all night and you will not get by'. In fact the only other mine was that which had blown up the German scout car at the entrance to Dinant.

The officer hesitated. The scout car had not returned. That they knew. The road could indeed be mined. They decided not to move. The long column divided and bivouacked in the nearby Mayenne woods. That is alleged to be why Celles was the furthest point reached by the Wehrmacht in Hitler's final gambler's throw for victory in the Second World War. The following morning wave after wave of American Lightnings pulverised the area.

Meanwhile Allied armoured columns were rolling forward. Two days after Christmas it was all over. The force which was to have recaptured Dinant was reeling in retreat to Rochefort. The Germans had looked on the Meuse for the last time. Dinant had been spared yet another destruction – and just by a few hours.

But to return to the present and the rusty tank outside the Café Ardennais. As Tony, my husband, was looking at it another car drew up near us and two men got out. Like us they were obviously disappointed to find the café closed and walked over to us. They were two Germans. One joined Tony in examining the tank with interest while the other said to me, 'My friend was in the army in the last war and was in a tank regiment'. 'What a coincidence,' I replied, 'my husband was also in the army, not in a tank regiment but in the gunners'. We all peered in through the café windows but could see no one and after shaking hands went our separate ways.

Later we heard that, according to the present owner, many Americans still stop for a drink and to take a snapshot of the tank. Madame Monique left sometime ago to open another café elsewhere. Was she really the saviour of Dinant? The local newspapers and a lot of people all said so, and why not? Of course there were many cynics who thought differently. Like the old fellow, survivor of two occupations, who said that in his opinion Marthe had warned the Germans against going further because, with the road blocked by the damaged tank, the others would have had to detour through her neat garden.

Two framed photographs, yellowing with age, still hang on the café wall. One shows plump little Marthe standing by the tank lying on its side. The other is of two British officers study-ing a map on the bonnet of a staff car outside the café. The sharp features of one of them beneath a black beret stir the memories of the older generation and, sure enough, at the bot-tom is the forceful autograph 'Montgomery of Alamein, Field Marshal'.

The Ardennes merge into the three provinces of Namur, Belgian Luxembourg and Liège so far as Belgium is concerned. Similar wooded, hilly country carries on into Germany – the Eiffel – and into the Duchy of Luxembourg and Northern France. It is possible that when Shakespeare was writing *As You Like It* he may have been thinking of the forest country between Marche and Laroche as a suitable place for his exiled Duke to live. 'They say he is already in the Forest of Arden and many merry men with him, and there they live like old Robin Hood of England, and fleet the time carelessly as they did in the Golden World'.

Laroche, deep in a lush valley, is a holiday centre with

numerous hotels of which one of the best is the small Air Pur with only 12 rooms. The restaurant is unique in the region and is mentioned in Relais de Campagne, among other distinguished guides. Mine host is Richard Cabouret and he would prefer the Michelin to mention the Air Pur as a restaurant rather than an hotel as he likes to keep his rooms for people who eat there. He attends to the hotel's administration and the cellar, his artistic wife does the décor and lovely flower arrangements and the chef, who served his apprenticeship at the Beau Rivage in Lausanne, produces the exquisite cooking with the aid of three commies. One way of serving trout is guaranteed to whet the curiosity as much as the appetite. It arrives at the table in the plastic bag in which it has been cooked. Pierced with a sharp knife this releases a delicious aroma as well as revealing the almond encrusted fish which literally melts in the mouth.

The river Ourthe flows through the centre of Laroche and is closely built up on both sides. Making blue earthenware is the outstanding local craft which is pretty and inexpensive to buy. Visitors can watch the potters at work in the Rue Rompre. Ardennes paté is obtainable in Britain in attractive bowls of this ware.

Laced with shady paths, wooded hills rise from the river banks with the romantic castle of the Counts de la Roche cresting a high hilltop. It is now in ruins but *Son et Lumière* brings the old castle and the people who lived there back to life, and, as always with such presentations, history and legend are inextricably mixed.

The saddest tale is that of the Countess Bertha's betrothal to a mysterious masked knight. Her father had promised her hand to the victor of a joust. Two knights came forward. One was the enormous Comte de Montaigu the other a slight figure in dark armour. To everyone's amazement the smaller knight vanquished the Comte. The stranger had won the hand of the rich heiress of the castle. Next day however instead of wedding bells there was tragedy when the corpse of the frail knight was found in the moat. It was that of Alix de Halm, the jilted fiancée of the faithless Montaigu, who, having had her revenge, had committed suicide.

The castle is surrounded by forests with deer and other woodland creatures. Hunting rules are rigidly observed in Belgium and since the Middle Ages saints were not only believed to ensure rich spoil but also to protect hunters from harm and injury. One of the most interesting miracles in the hunting world is told of Saint Hubert who lived at the beginning of the eighth century in Aquitania. He spent his youth at the court of the Franconian King where he indulged in wordly pleasures and passionately loved the chase. He continued his mode of life even after he had become the ruler of Aquitania. Seven different lives of the saint have been recorded so it is uncertain when he came to Belgium but one Good Friday, when he was chasing deer in the Ardennes, there appeared before him a stag with a luminous cross between its antlers. In a human voice it is said to have rebuked him for the way he lived. From that day on he repented and exchanged his worldly life for a spiritual one. He died in 728 when he was the Bishop of Liège and his body was buried in a monastery in the Ardennes not far from the place where the miracle occurred. During one of Belgium's invasions the saint's precious bones were hidden and have never been found. Saint Hubert became the patron saint of hunters and gamekeepers and several orders of knighthood have been under his protection. His memory is honoured on 3 November and this day is a favourite one for big hunts.

The Order of Saint Hubert gave hunting a nobler meaning than the killing of animals and membership was a great honour sought by most feudal lords. The cult of the saint is still such that pilgrims come to the town of his name every year to attend a special open-air mass which includes a fanfare of hunting horns.

The main building in the town of Saint Hubert is the basilica of the saint which was built between 1526 and 1564. The marble lining of the chair and the pillars were constructed during following years. In 1797 the church was stripped of its bells, wrought iron gates and its most precious ornaments. In 1847 King

Leopold I made a gift of the cenotaph of Saint Hubert created by the sculptor Guillaume Geefs. In the same year the Province of Luxembourg presented a picture of the saint's conversion by Lambert Mathieu. Excavations in 1956 uncovered foundations of the Morovingian and Romanesque churches which had existed on the site.

The high altar is 55 feet high and the altar of Saint Hubert in one of the side chapels has a tableau representing the consecration of the saint by Pope Serge I. The tabernacle contains a reliquary given in 1873 by the diocese of Liège.

In the wall opposite the altar there are rings where victims of rabies supposedly awaiting a cure were chained, for Saint Hubert's blessing was also invoked for hydrophobia. It is said that tiny threads from his stole were inserted into their foreheads to help them recover. The stole is kept in the treasury with other relics such as the chasuble said to have belonged to Charlemagne.

Bouillon is for some visitors the *pièce de résistance* of the Ardennes forest tour. You can drive from Saint Hubert to Paliseul. Then through wooded country and over hills down to the Semois river where Bouillon edges both banks while Godfrey de Bouillon's castle watches over the town. The great crusader mortgaged his property to the Archbishop of Liège in 1095 to pay for his expedition in the First Crusade. His humility as a Christian was such that he refused the crown offered to him as King of Jerusalem, saying that he could not wear a crown of gold when our Lord wore a crown of thorns.

In the castle you can see the famous stone bench where Godfrey would sit with an aide and watch through a lookout hewn out of the rock from which he could see the road to Liège and the one leading from France at the same time. A wooden cross has been uncovered as recently as 1963. It is lodged in a crack in the ground. There are labyrinths of corridors, underground passages, dungeons and great halls indicative of past strife and fighting but also of greatness.

Many distinguished people have visited Bouillon; Victor Hugo was one and another was Napoleon III who, after the French defeat of Sedan 10 miles away, spent the night of 3 September 1870 in the Hotel de la Poste. The hotel overlooks the river beside a little bridge and from the dining room you can get a magnificent view of the Semois with the castle high on the opposite bank. The manager, Raymond Bonvin, has been there for 29 years since he left the Palace Hotel in Brussels. Although he is now in his 70s he is as spry as a young man and seems to be everywhere at once so the hotel runs like clockwork.

Bastogne is another well-known town in the province of Luxembourg. Just before Christmas 1944 the Germans delivered an ultimatum to the American forces defending the town. A blindfolded German officer was led to General McAuliffe's cellar headquarters where he offered the alternatives of unconditional surrender or annihilation. He received the now famous reply, 'Nuts'. In the ensuing 'Battle of the Bulge', Von Rundstedt's last offensive of Hitler's war, a third of Bastogne was indeed shattered before General Patton's troops relieved it.

You can read the dramatic story of those grim December days of 1944 engraved in gold on the inner walls of the Mardasson Memorial, a mile away from the town. High on a knoll in the midst of green fields the Memorial is in the form of a five-pointed star.

8. The Province of Liège

Liège is the capital of the province of the same name and until the nineteenth century bore resemblance to Venice. It first made its appearance in history about 558 when Saint Monulph, Bishop of Tongres, built a chapel near the confluence of the Meuse and Legia rivers. During the following century a small town grew up around it and Saint Lambert, another Bishop of Tongres, moved there. He was assassinated and his successor Saint Hubert built another church over the tomb of the martyred bishop about 720, making Liège also his residence. From 972-1008 it became the episcopate of Notger acquiring more land and the saying grew up 'Liège owes Notger to God, and everything else to Notger'.

Geographically this section of the country is flat. Centuries ago the Meuse fingered its way in streams and tributaries over the plateau and higher ground became a series of islands. The latter were built up and connected by shop-lined bridges. So Liège grew in a valley protected by hills and industry prospered. Lagoons and streams reflected factories and steeples and the town became known not only for its all-powerful Prince-Bishops but for its coal, iron, marble, zinc and lead.

Arrogant and wordly, the Prince-Bishops' wealth increased. They relied on the aid of the Emperor and the Brabant counts to repress citizens who smarted under their exorbitant taxes. 'The Wild Boar of the Ardennes', William de la Marck, murdered one Prince-Bishop, exposed his naked body in front of Saint Lambert's Cathedral and donned the Prince-Bishop's mitre himself.

He in turn was later beheaded by order of Maximilian and the Prince-Bishops continued to wield great power in Liège.

Today the town retains little of its old Venetian aspect. The lagoons and streams have been filled in and made into broad city boulevards but their names such as 'Sovereign Bridge', 'Island Bridge' and 'Under Water' evoke the past. The Meuse, as always, flows through the centre of the city. New buildings, like the vast modern Congress Building and Holiday Inn, soar on the margins of the river.

The university is one of the largest in the country and the law courts are installed in the old palace of the Prince-Bishops. This sixteenth-century building is most impressive with two court-yards. Open galleries surround the first one supported by 60 columns, each of different design. The second has a central ornamental pool and gay flower beds. The palace interior is hung with Brussels tapestries. A wide staircase leads upwards to lavishly furnished chambers. On one landing a portrait of a Prince-Bishop stares at you. He wears a gold lamé cloak and there is a small pineapple close to his left hand. The pineapple is symbolic of Liège and you will see it in many places and on the city's coat of arms. It signifies solidarity.

César Franck was born here in 1822. A monument to his memory was presented to the town by French musicians in 1922 and stands in the foyer of the Liège Academy of Music. The Academy's concert hall can seat 1,700 and the width of the stage is equal to that of the Paris Opera House.

Grétry Square is named after another Liège musician André Ernest Modeste Grétry, who also spent many of his years in France. He became a leading composer of comic opera and travelled widely making acquaintances of such controversial figures as Voltaire. One of his masterpieces, 'Richard Coeur de Lion', became connected with a great historic event in an indirect way because the expression of loyalty contained in some of its music was answered by the popular anthem 'Le Marseillaise'. Napoleon bestowed the Cross of the Legion of Honour and a pension on him. Fifteen years after the composer died at the

Hermitage in Montmorency, formerly the house of Rousseau, his heart was reburied in Liège.

The Theatre Royal stands on one side of Grétry Square. Its façade contains eight marble columns with unusual cast iron bases and capitols which once decorated the church of the Carthusians. A statue of the musician, right hand placed inside his long coat as if on his heart, is erected with the back to the theatre. The plinth beneath the figure contains an urn where the illustrious musician's heart rests.

In 1587 Ernest of Bavaria, the son of the Duke of Bavaria, was elected Prince-Bishop and became the first of a dynasty which, descending from uncle to nephew, ruled the principality until 1723 and succeeded in maintaining its neutrality even though the neighbouring countries were at war.

This was the golden age of the Liège gunsmiths. In the seventeenth century they numbered over 7,000, and supplied arms to all countries, especially to Peter the Great's Russia, to England and many German principalities. In the eighteenth century arms were dispatched to the United Provinces, Portugal, Spain and many other countries. In 1778 there were 80 gunsmiths who made no fewer than 200,000 guns every year. By the nineteenth century there were close on 150 master gunsmiths in the city. In 1850, production rose to 600,000 units and in 1907, 1,580,000 – a record figure that has never been equalled since.

In order to protect the reputation of the Liège arms industry, Prince-Bishop Maximilian-Henry of Bavaria issued a decree on 10 May 1672, instituting a test house. In addition he stipulated that arms manufactured in the principality must be tested there and this is still done today. In addition to army weapons, sporting guns were perfected over the years and the gunsmiths soon became masters of the art of engraving.

The story is brought up to date by the arrival of the American inventor John M. Browning to develop the shot gun turned down by Remington and Winchester in the United States of America. He went on to devise automatic pistols, rifles and machine guns and today the Fabrique Nationale (FN) is one of the foremost producers of small arms, exporting all over the world.

Like Manchester with its Ship Canal, Liège has its narrower Albert Canal which gives small sea-going vessels and barges access to Antwerp and the sea.

There are many good hotels in Liège, usually adjoining excellent restaurants. Two American-sponsored ones in near de luxe category are the Ramada Inn, Boulevard de la Sauvenière and the Holiday Inn, Rue du Parc, across the Meuse river.

The English Trust Houses Forte chain have a new Post House with 100 bedrooms about one and a half miles to the west of the river Meuse, along the E5 autoroute which links Belgium with Germany. It is reached by taking the exit from the autoroute marked 'Herstal', 'Plateau Hauts Sarts', and is 57 miles from Brussels and just five and a half miles from the Dutch frontier. The overall management is in the capable hands of Dutch-born Robert Van Wijz, an international hotelier and son of the owner of the well-known 'Hotel du Casque' at Maastricht. The sliding glass doors of the restaurant open on to a terrace with a view over a wooded valley and an open-air heated swimming pool.

Spa, some 15 miles south east of Liège, has had its name incorporated into English as meaning a watering place, for it was the forerunner of them all. It was the first place in Europe to develop its natural springs for medicinal purposes and, before the First World War, the aristocracy flocked there to 'take the cure' in various ways from drinking the rather nauseous water to wallowing in the mud. It became the thing to do for rheumatic diseases or respiratory ailments – indeed was so fashionable that people in perfect health considered it the smart place for a holiday.

Spa was first mentioned by Pliny the Elder who told of the healing powers of its springs but it is said to have been a blacksmith from Breda who rediscovered its waters and bought a forest clearing near the springs (pouhons) from one of the Liège Prince-Bishops. Peter the Great of Russia visited Spa and since that time the main spring has been called 'Pouhon Peter the

Great'. Gustavus III of Sweden and Joseph II of Austria also used it and the Venetian Agostino, who was Henry VIII's physician, was the first doctor to prescribe the waters for treatment of rheumatism.

In 1654 the exiled King Charles II stayed in Spa with his sister, the Princess of Orange. According to a local biographer:

> When it was known that Charles II was coming to Spa, a great quantity of noblemen from the Low Countries and elsewhere set out for the little town and there were countless entertainments. The Prince's character afforded a peculiar blend of religious ideas, wordly tastes, and a propensity for pleasure . . . He was tall and had a fine figure.

Doctor Nessel, author of a book on mineral waters from Spa in 1713, stated that the English were great connoisseurs of the springs and considered they were a gift bestowed by nature. Export of the water to England boomed. An English agent in Rotterdam had bottles of it shipped across the Channel. Average orders from British merchants were 50 hampers of 160 bottles each. On 10 May 1733, Henry Eyre, purveyor to HM the Queen of England of Spa Waters, was granted exclusive rights to have the royal coat of arms with the words 'Pouhon in Spa' on the neck of each bottle.

The life of the little Ardennes town became influenced by the English in every respect. A race course was built and horse-racing was attended by Dukes and Lords from England and Ireland. On 10 January 1781 the second son of King George III travelled to Spa under the name of Count Hoya on his way to Osnabruck to take possession of the bishopric.

The ex-Empress of France, Josephine, on her way to Spa in 1811 was stopped by a constable who told her to turn back and when she indignantly asked why he replied – 'Madam, Spa is an entirely English town!'

After the battle of Waterloo the Duke and Duchess of Cumberland and the Duke of Wellington visited Spa. Perhaps the latter came because English soldiers discovered a book called *Les Amusements de Spa* amongst Napoleon's baggage. As well as the race course there was gambling at an elegant casino where visitors played for jewellery as well as money in various denominations.

Spa reached its zenith as a rendezvous of international society during the eighteenth and nineteenth centuries. Gambling became more popular than taking the waters and in 1751 the Liège Prince-Bishop, Jean Theodor, granted the gaming monopoly of the casino to a Scotsman who made a fortune. Other gaming houses sprang to life, the Redoute, the Levoz and the Vauxhall.

Down through the years Spa has not only retained its curative springs and famous casino but a historical mystique. The Kaiser had his headquarters at Spa in 1918 and had an underground concrete shelter built at Neubois castle. It was in Spa that he abdicated. After the armistice Foch, Hoover and Pershing stayed there while preliminary meetings were held for the armistice. In 1920 Lord Curzon and Lloyd George arrived for the Peace Conference. Lloyd George was asked to open the beautiful golf course at Malchamps. A personal gift was made to the town by Major C. R. Radcliff in the Parc de Sept Heures. This is a translation of the dedication in French on the armistice monument:

> In remembrance of the victory of the Allies and in homage, respect and admiration for the suffering of gallant Belgium, this monument is offered to the town of Spa by an English officer.

Edged with pine forests, boasting many hotels, elegant villas, its casino and lovely Lake Warfaz, Spa is still an enticing tourist halt in the Ardennes. The golf course is one of the most attractive in the country. In the centre of the town the wide Avenue Reine Astrid, ablaze with begonias, is a colourful background for pavement cafés. In mid August the 'Battle of Flowers' is reminiscent of that held at Nice. As in the past visitors can watch the famous Spa water being bottled but today it takes place in the ultra-modern bottling plant of Spa Monopole. There are guided tours daily during the summer.

A forest clearing on the outskirts of Spa has provided a small airfield. On the way to Stavelot the Francorchamps circuit is used for car and motorcycle racing during the season. Close by is the 'Cascade de Coo' a double waterfall thundering under a bridge in rainbows of spray. The little town of Coo has grown up with small inns where, if you cannot spend the night, you must at least sample the delectable *truite d'Ambleve avec des points noirs* – truly a delicacy.

At Sauvenière there is a spring which has a stone to one side which is said to bear the footprint of Saint Remacle. If a childless woman places her foot in this she may become pregnant. One guide remarked that this was often true in the old days when there were plenty of monks around the place !

Not far from Stavelot there is the charming little town of Malmédy which was annexed to Prussia in 1815 but remained Walloon in language, customs and sentiment. The Treaty of Versailles restored it to Belgium together with the district of Eupen. During the First World War its position was delicate to say the least. A war memorial bears an uncontroversial inscription and, though the town was again razed to the ground in the Von Rundstedt offensive of the Second World War, the memorial was not destroyed.

Malmédy possesses mineral springs which, like those at Spa, are called pouhons; also as at Spa, the waters are bottled and exported. The town is situated on the river Warche and is unusual in many ways, one being that it is completely surrounded by another village. This explains why, in such a small place, there are two town halls close together. Woe betide the stranger who mistakes one for the other! The soil is geologically distinct from that of the rest of the Ardennes, being of more recent formation. It consists of Triassic sandstone, in which the brooks and streams have cut picturesque ravines.

In the immediate neighbourhood there are many pleasant walks. The river Warchenne flows through the charming Mon

21 *In the centre of Luxembourg city*

Bijou Park to join the Warche which is flanked by high wooded hills. Paths lead to Baroque Michel, an ancient castle, and there are benches from which you can enjoy wonderful views. But perhaps for the visitor the most satisfying walk is through forest land up a mountain track to the Ferme Libert, a family hotel on the hilltop. There you can rest, and have a glass of beer or wine before going back to Malmédy. If you are hungry there are the special Malmédy waffles that have small hearts imprinted on the top instead of the usual criss-cross decoration. The hotel has several bedrooms and the walks from here are delightful. There is a more luxurious sister hotel further down the valley, the Hotel Maison Geron. If you are staying in Malmédy itself this is a delightful place for an evening meal.

Malmédy is best known for its carnival, held just before Lent, which is one of the merriest in Belgium. Bands play all day and the main square is crowded with people from early morning. Even the usual sedate city fathers don large ostrich-plumed hats and long colourful cloaks. Throughout the day the cafés are full of people coming and going. Everyone wears carnival costumes, even the smallest child. Do not bother to have your hair specially done for the day as the local lads carry long wooden arms with fingers attached to ruffle people's hair. Everyone awaits the big moment, the start of the parade. It has many bands and stretches seemingly for miles. Floats go by depicting scenes from fairy tales or historic events. Young men in smocks and knitted caps, wearing long-nosed masks go about in sixes. The leader will follow a stranger and copy his every gesture while the other five will copy their leader. Onlookers are drawn into the mêlée and the fun goes on until sunset.

Eupen is also known for its carnival festivities just before Lent. The preparation for this annual event begins on the first Sunday after 11 November. Topical and burlesque ballets are practised as are songs and music. Costumes are made, floats designed and, most important of all, the Carnival Prince must be chosen by secret ballot.

The Sunday before the big day the children's carnival is held.

22 *Unveiling of Churchill statue in Luxembourg city, 1973*

Streets and squares are crowded with swarms of children in different disguises blowing trumpets and whistles and playing drums. Confetti rains down on young and old alike. The following day is 'Rosenmontag' (Rose Monday) when the grown ups take over. The name derives from an ancient custom of throwing paper roses into the crowds during the parade.

About 10 o'clock in the morning the handsome Carnival Prince in doublet and hose, flowing cloak and plumed hat in green, white and gold, accompanied by his entourage of Lords and Ladies, arrives at the Town Hall in a sleek motor car decorated as a coach. The Mayor bestows all powers on him for the duration of the feast day and he is then acclaimed from the Town Hall balcony by a cheering crowd. After this the Prince departs to take his place in the parade, which is a splendid affair. Some 50 floats mounted on trucks and cars slowly make their way through admiring crowds and costumed figures march in time to the many bands. The parade takes about two hours to pass and then everyone repairs to the cafés and restaurants to eat and drink. Rosenmontag ends with a costume ball at night to wind up the proceedings until the following year.

Eupen itself has other attractions besides its carnival including fine old eighteenth-century patrician houses, built by cloth manufacturers whose ancestors came from the Ghent area. The parish church of Saint Nicolas dates back originally from 1727 and contains interesting works of art, among them a remarkable thirteenth-century Virgin. Above the town on the river Vesdre is Belgium's largest dam – 207 feet high and over 1,300 feet long.

9. The Campine and Limburg

The Campine, which includes parts of Antwerp and Limburg provinces, stretches from the Scheldt to the Meuse. The Flemish-speaking people of this sandy moorland region have farmed for centuries and in recent times the discovery of coal and cutting of the Albert Canal have enriched the area. The small town of Mol is the centre of Belgium's atomic energy industry but there is still a tranquil, medieval atmosphere in such places as Diest and Lier and some of Belgium's oldest towns are to be found in the region. It also contains two of the largest museums in Europe, the Provincial motor car museum at Houthalen and the open-air folk village at Bokrijk, reminiscent of those in Ireland and Denmark.

At Bokrijk, an old-time village of the type which Breughel depicted so well, has been set up on a 75-acre nature reserve half way to Genk. The work was started in 1958. Ancient farm houses have been reassembled and thatched, antique peasant furniture and kitchen copper ware collected, an old windmill is the focal point and real farm animals add to the bucolic charm. The picture is completed by people dressed in peasant costume of the day, wandering around and even indulging in farming activities; altogether a very relaxing and quiet visit, well worth making in our modern bustling world.

Genk, a few miles from Bokrijk, is a holiday resort of lakes and forests with an open-air theatre. Sint Truiden, founded in the seventeenth century, has the second largest market place in Belgium and is well known for its cherry orchards.

Diest, tucked into a triangle between the provinces of Antwerp, Brabant and Limburg, is a good tourist stop with several hotels and restaurants. Part of its medieval ramparts are still intact and the cobbled streets of its beguinage can be entered through a fine Baroque gateway. A statue of the Virgin and Child is in the niche overhead. Mary wears a golden crown and looks down over the shoulders of the Christ child at the passers-by below. Quaint little sixteenth- and seventeenth-century houses line the quiet beguinage streets, there are two ancient breweries, unfortunately no longer operating, and there is a fourteenth-century Gothic church dedicated to Saint Catherine which has some lovely wooden carvings. The beguinage, founded in 1252, is no longer consecrated and, as is so often said in Belgium, remains 'a small town within a town'.

The other great attraction in Diest, besides its modern sports centre, is the main square. Its seventeenth-century houses with stepped gables make a suitable backing for the late-Gothic Church of Saint Sulpice and the Town Hall. The church has a carillon of 43 bells.

The Town Hall has a unique museum which is in three cellars discovered after damage during the last war. They are at different levels and are linked by three doorways. Illuminated niches in the brick walls hold various exhibits such as carved wooden statues of saints from the beguinage including one of Saint Barbara, the patron saint of artillery. Draped over the shoulders of the latter is a real red velvet cloak edged with gold lace. Beneath Gothic arches suits of armour are cunningly lit and several paintings are also well displayed. One shows William the Silent's son, Phillip William, who is buried in the Church of Saint Sulpice – the only royal prince of the Netherlands to be buried outside Holland. The painting depicts him lying in state. About the bier, surrounded by gigantic candles, stand priests with folded arms.

At one time three local guilds ruled the town and you can see a wooden chest which used to contain the town documents. It has three keyholes so a member of each of the three guilds had to be present whenever it was opened, as in modern banks. There are many crossbows for archery was a great pastime in Diest and to be the president of the Archers' Guild was a high honour. This was decided by quaffing goblets of ale and the man who could drink the most while standing on one leg was elected.

Not far from Diest are the Norbertine abbeys of Averbode and Tongerlo. Both have had serious fires in recent times but have been rebuilt. Averbode, some seven miles from Diest and approached through a wooded avenue, is one of Europe's most important monasteries. Its restored buildings reflect the very modern outlook of the brothers. Religion here is practical and very much in contact with the outside world. Visitors are welcome, especially youth groups and students studying for exams for whom board and lodging can be provided.

From the twelfth century stress has been laid at Averbode on the written word and the abbey printing works produces many colour magazines for children among other publications in Flemish and German.

The Abbot's House is interesting. The dining room walls are of tooled leather salvaged from the fires. In the music room is one of the abbey treasures, a great embossed plate by Rubens. It hangs, like a plaque, on the wall and was used at one time to offer the keys of the city to visiting dignitaries. It is some four feet in diameter and shows a man on a galloping horse so life-like that one is reminded of Reynold's remark about Rubens' paintings of these animals : 'His horses are perfect in their kind'.

Until 1802 the abbey was in the Liège diocese and subject to the Prince-Bishops there. It was also astride the Brabant frontier which sometimes posed delicate problems. Later it was transferred to Malines diocese. Abbeys have their own rules about eating and drinking. Probably the reason why monks are usually portrayed as plump is because some monasteries insist on a farinaceous diet. Others allow fish on certain days and sometimes meat. The rules also differ on the subject of drinking. At Averbode the monks may smoke at any time and can drink wine and beer on Sundays. The monks at Orval in the south east of Belgium make a famous beer, a dark, potent brew which they serve to visitors with delicious cheese and crusty brown bread. You can order this beer or that of several other monasteries in many restaurants throughout Belgium where it is called 'Trappiste'.

Tongerlo Abbey, 42 miles from Antwerp and 37 north east of Brussels, has two categories of monks. The canons, whose robes are white like those at Averbode, and the lay brothers who wear a grey mantle and must also grow a beard. The main task of the latter is the manual labour, particularly for the monastery farm. Though silence and fasting are rules, because of the hard work they are not rigidly enforced. A mission was founded in 1898 by Tongerlo for the Congo and, by the middle of the century, half the community was working there.

A painting of Da Vinci's 'Last Supper' copied by Andrea Solario, a pupil of the master, is the abbey's greatest treasure. It covers the entire wall of a concrete and glass theatre built especially for it in 1966. It is possible that the great artist himself may have painted in details and outlines but this is not known for certain. Before the turn of the century the painting was sent to London for sale as the abbey was in financial difficulties but it did not reach the reserved price and was returned. While a monk shows the painting and explains the above story the audience in the theatre usually maintains an awed silence but, on the occasion of my visit, I enjoyed the remark of a gentleman sitting near me. Correctly addressed in a transatlantic drawl I heard – 'Oh, brother! Try Sotheby's now!' The monk paused in his explanation and said, 'Did I hear someone call out "Oh Brother?" Is there anything I can do?'

Lier lies ten miles south east of Antwerp and is one of the prettiest towns in Belgium. As long ago as the thirteenth century it was described as a 'little Paradise'. You enter it over a bridge and the course of the river Nethe is so capricious that almost all the town is by the riverside. It has a charming Grand Place where the elegant Town Hall built during the eighteenth century, has over 3,500 window panes of bottle green glass. Inside, the chambers and halls are beautifully proportioned and the square entrance hall has an intricately carved wooden staircase.

Left of the Town Hall is a slender belfry with ornate finials. In complete contrast the flamboyant Church of Saint Gommaire has a massive tower containing a carillon. There is a very fine roodscreen and the stained-glass windows in the choir depict Emperor Maximilian, Mary of Burgundy and their children and are called the 'Royal Windows'. An interesting triptych in one of the chapels in the apse is partly the work of Rubens and a delightful window in the south transept is of the Virgin Mary being crowned.

Another attraction of Lier is a medieval defence tower, a relic of the city's old fortifications which might have been designed by Hans Christian Andersen for one of his fairy tales. This is known as the Zimmer Tower because it now houses a unique clock designed by a local clockmaker, Louis Zimmer. The giant face is in fact 13 dials comprising a normal one in the middle surrounded by 12 more which provide a mass of astronomical information. Four figures in niches strike the quarters, halves and hours. Zimmer was born in Lier in 1888 and became clockmaker to the King of the Belgians. He designed the Centenary Clock on the occasion of the 100th anniversary of Belgium's independence, as one of Belgium's exhibits at the New York World Exhibition in 1939. Later he produced his second masterpiece which is housed in a building at the base of the tower: an astronomical clock which has 93 dials and 14 automatons. There is an auditorium in which lectures are given explaining the working of the mechanism and it is well worth a visit for the mechanically-minded.

The beguinage is in the south of the town. It covers some five acres and contains several hundred tiny houses. Behind it flows the Nethe. The entrance gate is of sober design with glassed-in niche containing a statue of the Virgin in red and blue robes and the Christ child in white. Mary holds a rosary in her hand. The lanes have unusual names such as 'Pump Alley' and 'Hell's Dead End'. Each house carries the name of a male or female saint or a symbol. Our guide told us that one beguine remained whose name was Agnes and that she lived in the house called

'Cornelius'. We hesitated outside a small doorway. 'How old is she?' inquired a member of the party. 'Sixty-seven' said the guide promptly and loudly. Agnes must have been just inside the hallway and heard the last remark. She opened the door and shooed us all away angrily. I suggested to the guide that if he made her age 10 years younger she might well have invited us in with a smile.

Perhaps Agnes' displeasure was a left-over from the past because the beguines at Lier had many problems. A conflict arose in 1258 when the beguines wished to have a church of their own and this caused resentment in the parish of Saint Gommaire.

Other differences arose in 1436 between the beguinage and its priest on one side and the chapter and parish priest of Saint Gommaire on the other. Certain women who were not beguines but who lived in the beguinage, remained, in the chapter's view, members of the parish and had to arrange to be buried, on their death, by the priest of the chapter and not by that of the beguinage. Each of the opposing parties had a financial interest in the dispute. There was still another problem : the discretion as to hours of service. The beguinage priest was not allowed to say mass before the priest of Saint Gommaire. One exception to this rule : the Good Friday service could be celebrated in both churches simultaneously. To compensate for the financial losses occasioned by its separate services, the beguinage had to pay the chapter a certain sum each year. Religious squabbling is indeed well established.

In strict contrast the town of Geel, further north, has been a place of understanding and compassion for centuries for it is here that the mentally disturbed are literally treated 'as one of the family'. Legend has it that, in the year AD 600, Dymphna, an Irish princess, was executed in Geel by her father. In consequence of certain miracles which she had effected she was afterwards canonized and made the patron saint of the insane. A Gothic church is dedicated to her and bears her name. Fine panel paintings representing incidents in her life are probably by a contemporary of Memling. Her relics are in a wooden shrine. The Geel system of helping the mentally sick, who have no homicidal tendencies, is humane and enlightened. It is basically a religious work though today it is paid for by families of the patients or indeed by the state. Local families welcome these people into their homes to become a member of the family. They advise and help them get local jobs and in the majority of cases this 'becoming part of the family' has produced the most amazing cures. If the waiter in a café is slow or perhaps the clerk in a bank is abrupt or someone serving in a shop shows little interest in what is bought, no one in Geel will complain or think it is strange. Behaviour of this kind has become a normal way of life for the inhabitants of Geel. The town is often affectionately referred to as the City of Charity.

Another exceptional town further north again than Geel is Turnhout, where it is said 'Cards are Trumps'. Playing cards have been made here for over 100 years. When Belgian products are thought of the words lace, diamonds, crystal and chocolates come to mind but certainly not playing cards. Yet one of the largest of the four card factories in Turnhout was founded in 1837 as a family business and, from such modest beginnings, now exports between five and seven million packs of playing cards annually.

A century ago playing cards were cut out of cardboard with scissors. Today the production has been automated. First the cardboard is covered with a coat of white paint and must be absolutely flawless and it is then cut into sheets of a certain size, ready for the printing process. Afterwards the sheets are given a protective coating that serves to set the colours and helps the cards to slide well. Then the sheets are glazed to stiffen their resistance to moisture, and a linen finish can be added for customers wanting this process.

A machine cuts the sheets lengthwise and the strips are arranged so that when they are cut crosswise later on, the individual cards appear in their proper order from 1 to 10 along with the face cards in every suit. A special file is used to round off the corners, which – an exclusively Belgian feature – are gilded.

These two operations are still done by hand. For luxury playing cards, real gold leaf is used. Finally the packs are fed into an automated packing machine which inserts them into boxes and seals them.

There are many variations of design and size. The Belgian face cards differ from the Dutch, French, English and American. Also some customers request special designs. The backs of the cards lend themselves to endless variations. Apart from the neutral back in geometrical designs of single colour, there are fancy backs of dancers, heads of horses or dogs, reproductions of old masters or modern paintings, in multiple colours.

Should you have a little extra time to spare in Turnhout you will find the Playing Card Museum a fascinating place. It is full of rare items such as ancient Chinese cards, old presses and cards from many parts of the world with extraordinary and often beautiful designs. Most interesting are the Fortune Playing Cards from various countries. It is also possible to buy packs of cards in the museum.

Part 2

Luxembourg

1. Culture and History

Luxembourg is the largest of the five small independent countries in Europe and certainly one of the most fascinating. It has a constitutional monarchy, is bordered by Belgium, France and Germany and is 51 miles long and 36 miles wide, exactly 999 square miles. The inevitable question visitors ask is – 'Couldn't you just add one more to make the country a round 1,000 square miles?' The answer is always the same, said with an amused smile: 'We did add another mile once but the people who lived in it could not speak the language so we gave it back!' Perhaps this is one of the explanations of the Luxembourg motto: 'We wish to remain what we are'. Actually a dialect called Letzeburgesch is spoken by 276,000 of Luxembourg's 348,000 citizens but it is not generally used as a written language. The people are great linguists, English is understood all over the country and nearly everyone speaks it.

Luxembourg forms a low plateau intersected by several valleys and is drained by the Moselle and its tributary the Sûre. The Grand Duchy is prosperous, peaceful and friendly with medieval castles on hilltops and trees everywhere, for forests cover a third of the country. The hills are threaded with rushing streams, waterfalls and cascades. Admittedly in the south west corner there are mines, blast furnaces and steel works but visitors will be unlikely to holiday there. Yet this corner is a main source of the country's wealth.

Aciéries Réunies de Burbach-Eich-Dudelange, a company known as Arbed, produces 90 per cent of Luxembourg's iron and steel and this accounts for 70 per cent of the exports. It also employs about 50 per cent of the industrial manpower. Arbed is Europe's third largest steel-producing firm. Not forgetting the country's great financial position as a tax haven, other sources of revenue are mining, iron ore, agriculture and wine.

The north eastern region of the country is known as 'Little Switzerland' and it could not be better named for, instead of great mountains, there are craggy, steep hills with swift-flowing torrents, pine trees and wild flowers, small valleys with hamlets and fruit orchards. Driving along the winding roads in September and October on sunny days is an experience not to be missed. The red and gold of autumn leaves intermingling with contrasting evergreens against a washed blue sky makes one long to be an artist.

To the west the country is larger and more open as it edges into the Ardennes. Rich farming land is to the south and lush vineyards face their German counterparts across the Moselle.

The cuisine, like the language, is a mixture of the surrounding countries yet also has its own specialities such as trout, pike and chicken cooked in wine, venison, smoked ham and pork. Sweetbreads are succulent served with a thin Béarnaise sauce and galantine of duck is a favourite dish. Of the many sweet desserts the one I like best is light-as-air chocolate mousse. One cooked cheese speciality is called Kachkéis and it is just that with a distinctive flavour. It is cooked with egg yolk, butter and water and some people add mustard when eating it.

Luxembourg *gras double* is similar in taste to Alsation *paté de foie gras.* Jellied sucking pig and sausages are delicious. If you see 'Riverfood' on the menu it usually means fresh pike or trout. During carnival time you can indulge in 'Puzzled thoughts', a special rich pastry.

Having its own vineyards, Luxembourg produces some really fine wines. Luxembourg Moselle can be plain or sparkling. Soon after the grapes are gathered all the cafés and restaurants offer the 'new wine' served by the glass. It is slightly cloudy and tastes like a fresh, innocent grape juice and is most refreshing, but do not be misled or drink too much for it is very potent. To return to a Swiss simile again, the white Luxembourg wine tastes very like the dry white wine from the Valais, beloved by Winston Churchill. Liqueurs are 'Mirabelle', a plum brandy, 'Kirsch', a cherry brandy, and 'Quetsch' made from small dark plums. The best-known beers are Mousel, Clausen and Diekirch.

When you enter Luxembourg from Belgium there are no frontier problems as there is a customs union. Belgian money is accepted anywhere in the Grand Duchy but it is as well to remember that this arrangement is not always reciprocated.

One of the country's best-known features is of course Radio Luxembourg which broadcasts programmes in five separate languages including English. Housed in the city of Luxembourg in a modern building, surrounded by green lawns, flower beds and trees, its transmitters are some miles outside. It seems strange that pop music should go out around the clock from this conservative, quiet little city. Foreign firms sponsor broadcasts on this privately owned station which has a wide audience all over Europe and there are many stories connected with it.

Lord 'Haw Haw', William Joyce, broadcast anti-British propaganda for the Nazis from there during the German occupation. He was apparently drunk to the point of incoherence when he made his last one, knowing all was lost, and it was never put out. After the war William Joyce was convicted of treason in London and hanged.

During General de Gaulle's period of forceful management of the French economy, the Luxembourg broadcasts were much more frank than the closely controlled French ones and this irritated the General. The directors were summoned to Paris and reminded that there was a great deal of French money invested in the station. The Luxembourgers replied that they could easily nationalize it if forced to do so and that was the end of the attempted censorship.

Radio Luxembourg's well-known orchestra gives a series of concerts each winter in the magnificent New Theatre in the capital. As it is paid for by the station no charge for admission is made in the usual way. You give a sum of money to the Red Cross and obtain a ticket. The concert seats are always full for the Luxembourgers are ardent music lovers. The Diplomatic Corps, visitors and local people book a long time ahead to be certain of tickets on the first night of the season, which is a very special affair. During the interval most of the fashionably-dressed audience make their way to the modern, spacious bar where the popping of champagne corks can easily be heard above the chatter of people greeting each other.

Of the arts most Luxembourgers put music first in the same way as the Czechs. Perhaps it is because both countries are land-locked. Again like Czechoslovakia every village has its band, choral society or orchestra and it is the exception to find a family where not a single member can play a musical instrument.

The Grand Duchy has its own Post Office and railway. By train Luxembourg is ten hours from London and by air one hour. Working hours are from eight o'clock in the morning to noon and from two o'clock in the afternoon until six.

The high European Central Building dominates the skyline of the capital. It houses the Secretariat of the European Parliament and for three months of the year is the meeting place of the Council of Ministers of the European Community.

Luxembourgers are very internationally minded and their homeland, as has often been remarked, is 'a small country with a great history', too long to go into here but it has some very interesting points.

During the feudal period, among the powerful families which were established between the Moselle and the Meuse was the illustrious House of the Ardennes believed to have been descended from Charlemagne. They had large domains and one of the youngest sons, Sigefroid, rebuilt a little fortress into the Castle of Lucilinburhue overlooking the valley of the Alzette. Such, it is said, was the beginning of the city of Luxembourg. Before going further there is a fable about the reason Sigefroid, first Count of Luxembourg, chose this particular place in AD 963.

One evening the Count was returning from a hunt in the Ardennes and, as he rode through the valley of the Alzette, he heard a clear, bell-like voice singing. The voice was as alluring as the one Ulysses' sailors heard which led them to become lotus eaters. The singing seemed to come from the sky and the Count looked upwards and saw the remains of an old castle. On a pinnacle of rock above what remained of the ramparts there was a girl in a diaphanous green robe. She was the most beautiful creature he had ever seen. It was Melusine, the fairy of the Alzette and, as the sun sank and colour suffused the sky, she vanished. The Count returned to the idyllic place evening after evening but Melusine was elusive. Finally he found her and beseeched her to marry him and she consented on two condi-tions : that she should never be forced to leave the hilltop and that on Saturdays she could leave him and not be followed. Sigefroid agreed and so the old ruined castle was rebuilt, the couple were married and life was sweet. Unhappily human nature stepped in at this point.

Sigefroid's knights were curious about his lovely wife and where she went on Saturdays. They made suspicious innuendoes to him about this and eventually persuaded him to follow her. This he did. Melusine walked down the valley with Sigefroid close behind her. She dived into the river and as the Count cried out she turned into a mermaid. Hearing his voice Melusine looked back at him. Realizing that her beloved Sigefroid had broken his promise, she vanished. Sigefroid had lost her for ever.

The story does not end there. It is said that Melusine is imprisoned in the rock from which she first emerged. Once every seven years she reappears on her rock pinnacle, sometimes as a lovely woman, other times as a serpent but always with a golden key in her mouth. If a knight could take this from her it would unlock her from the spell that confines her to the rock. Be that as it may Sigefroid had the castle rebuilt and his entourage and vassals dwelt around the keep and the valley was cultivated. Such was the beginning of Luxembourg. An encircling wall with seven square towers and a moat surrounded the new born community and later it gave its name to the whole country.

Sigefroid's dynasty lasted for several generations and their territory grew. Later the romantic figure, John the Blind, had a special relationship with the English. He was a handsome and chivalrous prince whose eyes unfortunately became infected while he was in Lithuania. A French physician whom he consulted treated them but with no result and other doctors only caused his sight to worsen. At Montpelier University they did more harm than good and John became totally blind.

John did not wish people to know of his disability and did not allow his affliction to interfere with his life any more than he could help. When he received homage from strangers he kept his eyes down as if reading a book. Despite his precautions it was soon apparent to everyone that he was blind and from that time he was known as John the Blind.

During the Hundred Years War when Edward III of England invaded France, Philip VI appealed to John the Blind for assistance. John departed from Luxembourg with his son Charles and some 500 knights. During the Battle of Crecy when the French army was known to have been vanquished, he demanded to be taken where the fighting was fiercest crying – 'Lead me forward so that I may strike at least one good blow with my sword!' Two knights laced their bridles on either side of his and galloped into the thick of the fighting where he met his death.

Chateaubriand, recounting the episode later, describes this heroic deed as a 'True miracle of fidelity and honour and a worthy crowning to such a life'.

After the fighting was over the Black Prince, son of King Edward, was walking over the battlefield and came across the body of the brave Luxembourger. The Prince, seeing that the blind ruler's armorial bearings were of three ostrich feathers with the motto '*Ich Dien*' and being full of admiration for his adversary, adopted the coat of arms for his own. This has been the crest of each Prince of Wales from that time.

The following day King Edward delivered the body of John

the Blind back to his son Charles. It was returned to Luxembourg
where in September 1346 it was laid to rest in the Abbey of
Altmunster as the Count had requested. Later the abbey was
destroyed but John the Blind's remains were rescued and placed
in different abbeys until eventually he was entombed in the
cathedral in the capital.

Luxembourg's Royal House for some time supplied monarchs
for Europe in the same way that Denmark was to do later and
the country, like Brabant, became a 'Duchy'. During Napoleon's
conquests he swept Luxembourg into his empire. He sweetened
the blow somewhat when he arrived in the capital. On receiving
the key of the city he returned it with a smile and said, 'The key
is in good hands. Take it back'.

After Napoleon's fall Luxembourg became a pawn in European politics. The Vienna Congress found it difficult to satisfy
the quarrelling monarchs. The King of Prussia demanded land
that belonged to the King of Holland. His wish was granted but
the Dutch king William 1 was furious and was given the Duchy
of Luxembourg to placate him. It became a Grand Duchy in
1815. It seemed an excellent idea to those who drew up the
treaty for Luxembourg could serve as a buffer state between
Prussia and France. William was asked for a solemn agreement
not to incorporate the Duchy into his own kingdom. He gave his
word and then broke it. When Belgium separated from Holland
it demanded the Duchy and, as no agreement was reached for
some time, the two governors ran affairs in their own way. William governed from the city of Luxembourg and Belgium from
Arlon. To make matters more complicated for the Duchy she was
economically tied to Prussia. Such a state of affairs could not continue and in 1867 the countries surrounding the Duchy granted
Luxembourg's independence and neutrality. Prussia went so
far as to state that Luxembourg's railways should never be used
for war purposes.

The cruel sword that fell in 1914 and again in 1940, with disregard for treaties, did not succeed in crushing the Duchy of
Luxembourg but the cost of freedom was so high it seemed only

*

a miracle could save the country and each time it did. Not for one moment did the people forget their motto 'We wish to remain what we are'.

In 1890, union with Holland ended and Duke Adolf of Nassau was proclaimed Grand Duke of Luxembourg. In reply to an address of the President of the Chamber he said :

> From this day forth I am like you a Luxembourger and that from the bottom of my heart. It is my sincere wish to work with you for the welfare and intellectual and moral progress of our common fatherland; for the development of her free institutions, as well as for the consolidation of her autonomy and her independence in the sight of Europe.

In spite of being 73 years old he took up his new role with enthusiasm. A constitutional sovereign, he was interested in everything and served the little country with devotion.

As he approached the end of his life, his son Prince William was given the title of Lieutenant Representative and carried out many of his father's duties. Grand Duke Adolf died at the age of 83 and his son succeeded him with the title William iv. He married Maria Anna de Braganza, daughter of the King of Portugal. When he had received the Constitutional Oath he ended his speech by saying :

> Tell all the Luxembourgers that my whole life belongs to your dear country. It is in this sense that I take for my own the proud motto of our Count John the Blind: '*Ich Dien*'.

One of William's daughtes, Maria Adelaide, a most beautiful girl, was later to become Grand Duchess. Her role during the First World War was fraught with difficulty and she was denounced in Berlin as being hostile to Germany. She abdicated in 1919 and died in her 29th year. Princess Charlotte, then aged 23, who was betrothed to Prince Felix de Bourbon-Parma, succeeded her. So it came about that one sister witnessed the agony of the First World War and the other the Second. In 1939

Princess Charlotte's son, Prince Jean, 18 years of age, was proclaimed heir to the Grand Duchy. In the same year there was a great celebration of the 1200th anniversary of the death of Saint Willibrord from Northumberland – but more about the saint later.

Again with complete disregard for treaties the Nazis swept through the Grand Duchy of Luxembourg and the Government went into exile. The Grand Duchess came to London and her husband Prince Felix and son Prince Jean joined the Allied Forces, Prince Jean becoming an officer in the Irish Guards. The Nazis seized the steel factories and drafted young men into the German army. Possessing no army of their own, thousands of Luxembourgers volunteered for the French and other Allied forces and 2,000 of them were to lose their lives.

Rundstedt's winter offensive in 1944 struck through Luxembourg, beginning in the north of the country. Leaving their belongings, panic-stricken refugees fled westward and southward. Many of those who stayed were shot or deported to German concentration camps. Towns were razed and the Nazi tanks rolled on. Just before Christmas General Patton blunted Rundstedt's thrust in the Luxembourg sector. Before the new year the Americans had freed the Duchy but at great cost. About 9,000 Americans lost their lives and were buried in Hamm, some three miles from the capital. Today in this American cemetery there are still 5,076 graves, the other soldiers' bodies having been removed by relatives and reburied in their home country. Simple Latin crosses mark the graves – some have the Star of David.

One cross, a short distance from the others, marks the grave of General George S. Patton, junior, who commanded the Third Army. Ironically enough he died in a motor-car accident in Germany a few months after the fighting had ceased. Yet it is where this controversial figure would have wished to remain, among his soldiers.

When Luxembourg was liberated the people's joy knew no bounds and, to add to their happiness, the hereditary Grand

Duke Jean and Prince Felix were among the first allied soldiers entering Luxembourg.

The Grand Duchess Charlotte had spent some time in America during the war and was never to forget the words Roosevelt had said to her in the White House. 'Do not worry, my child, we will bring you back to Luxembourg'. His death was a grievous loss. In the President's honour the capital of Luxembourg named its finest boulevard after him.

The present ruler, the Grand Duke Jean, succeeded to the throne in November 1964, when his mother the Grand Duchess Charlotte abdicated. He is married to the Princess Josephine Charlotte of Belgium, sister of King Baudouin. They have five children, the Princes Henri, Jean and Guillaume, and the Princesses Marie-Astrid and Margarethe.

The executive power of the country is in the hands of the Grand Duke and a Cabinet of eight ministers. The legislative power rests with a Chamber of Deputies, elected by men and women over 18 years of age. There are four constituencies. The number of members of Parliament is based on population figures allowing one member for each 5,500 inhabitants. Bills are submitted to the 21-member Council of State, appointed by the sovereign.

Some 95 per cent of the population is Roman Catholic. Wayside shrines are dotted over the hills usually decorated with flowers during the summer season. Freedom of worship is traditional. Roman Catholic priests, Protestant pastors and Jewish rabbis are paid salaries by the state.

By tradition church bells do not ring from Good Friday to Easter Sunday. It is said that they have flown to Rome to confess. During these three days children go around with clappers to call people to church. On Candlemas Eve, in the same way as children 'trick or treat' at Halloween, Luxembourg boys and girls go around to call on houses, sing songs and are given fruit or chocolates.

2. Luxembourg City

The cosmopolitan little city of Luxembourg is fascinating. It has 90,000 inhabitants and, despite its new role as the banking centre of the European Economic Community, it has a delightful medieval atmosphere. Like Budapest it is divided into the 'Old' town and the 'New' town, only instead of being separated by a river it is divided by a deep canyon. The 'Old' part has often been referred to in the past as 'the Gibraltar of the North' for at one time it merely consisted of Sigefroid's great castle built in and around a rocky crag surrounded by three lines of defence. These consisted of 53 forts linked by 16 miles of tunnels and casements. Ten gates controlled admittance into this great citadel which covered 440 acres. At its base a gorge curved away into the valley of the Alzette.

The 'Old' town which grew up around the ancient fortress area has several bridges spanning the gorge to the 'New' part of the city. The best known is the Pont Adolphe beneath which the Petrusse river winds through green parkland. The busy Boulevard Roosevelt curves from the end of the Pont Adolphe past the cathedral with its three slender spires to another great viaduct from which there is also a fine view of the canyon dividing the city.

The cathedral has been converted from a former seventeenth-century Jesuit church and, like the city, is half old and half new. Much of the interior, such as the stained-glass windows and choir, is recent. The sarcophagus of John the Blind is in a chapel in the crypt. The royal family vault, designed in blue and gold mosaic, is also here. The cathedral is dedicated to the Virgin Mary, 'Our Lady of Luxembourg', and in May, from the third to the fifth Sunday after Easter, people make a pilgrimage from all over the country to pay her homage and pray for her continued protection. At the close of the ceremony the statue of the Madonna is taken from the cathedral and carried in procession to flower-decorated altars in various parts of the city. This religious event is known as the Octave.

Behind the cathedral runs the Grand Rue, a main street with lots of little shops and boutiques. Close by is the Place d'Armes, a charming square fringed with lime trees with a bandstand in the centre. There are all kinds of cafés. Le Cellier serves cheese, biscuits and wine to suit various tastes. La Marmite has more substantial meals. Le Rendezvous is strictly a snack bar and there are other places which you can investigate. In the square itself there are benches scattered about where people can sit and listen to the music of the 'Garde Ducale' band which plays there on certain days. During the summertime when open-air cafés come into their own it is a pleasant place to stop for a cooling drink. One called 'Apéritif Concert' is especially delicious but the ingredients are a secret. Cars are not allowed to park.

A few minutes' walk leads into a neighbouring square, the Place Guillaume, with a statue of William II, one of the most popular sovereigns of Luxembourg, in the centre. He is in full dress uniform astride his horse and holds his hat in his right hand as if greeting onlookers. He is backed by the Town Hall where two white stone lions guard the entrance steps.

In this same square there is an enchanting statue of Renert the Fox. It is over a memorial to Michel Rodange who wrote an epic poem about this animal regarded as a landmark in Luxembourg literature. The fox's cunning is proverbial. He has acted as a central character in fables from earliest times. His name 'Renert' means 'strong in council'. Animals differ as much as humans in their way of life. It is curious that the fox's eating habits are so unlike other creatures and that he is particularly partial to grapes yet will never eat the flesh of a bird of prey. Michel Rodange's Renert runs true to type in that he usually manages to outwit his enemies. His successful exploits in Rodange's poem are as well known to Luxembourgers as Hans Christian Andersen's tales are to the Danes. The Michel Rodange memorial is in the form of a white fountain. Above the water there is a medallion of the poet's head surrounded by a swag of laurel leaves. On a plinth at the top sits Renert, gazing down over his creator into the fountain. His ears are cocked and his body alert, he knows just what goes on in the Place Guillaume, especially on Wednesday and Saturday mornings when it is very crowded and there is a vegetable and flower market.

The Ducal Palace close by was once the Town Hall and, being cheek-by-jowl with other buildings, you could miss it except for the white gloved soldier in his grey sentry box. It is a pleasant mansion in the Spanish-French style and the extension of the building on the right side houses the parliament.

Being a small city like Bruges, all the interesting places in the centre are within walking distance. Narrow cobbled streets and shortage of parking spaces makes a car an embarrassment for the sightseer. It is much more rewarding to navigate with one of the excellent town maps and you will see some unique things which you would miss if driving. Away from the centre of the town, as in most capitals, this does not apply.

Modern Luxembourg lies around the area near the main railway station and the Avenue de la Liberté, a wide four-lane thoroughfare lined with trees, shops and offices. Here also you will see numerous banks, hotels and restaurants.

The Marché aux Poissons is the town's most ancient square with some lovely houses. It also boasts the oldest café which is in a building with a pillared front and is called appropriately, 'Under the Pillars'. Narrow lanes lead off the square in all directions. Here you can visit the National Museum. It is open daily except Mondays (10 – 12 a.m. and 2– 6 p.m.) and entrance is free.

The exhibits are well lit and displayed and include sculpture, paintings and a model of the city stronghold as it was during the Middle Ages. The museum has a section of natural history and archaeological, folklore and artistic collections.

It is said jokingly that you cannot go anywhere in the capital without crossing a bridge. There is a grain of truth in this as there are over 60, spanning steep-sided valleys in which flow the winding Alzette and Petrusse rivers. A good view over part of the city is afforded by a tour of the Bock Casemates, part of the old fortifications, which are open during the summer season. Turning left from the cathedral porch and left again in Rue Chimay will bring you to the Place de la Constitution and to the entrance. The main passages and gates are closed but about 14 miles remain; some of them have several floors connected by deep staircases which descend more than 120 feet. During the last two World Wars they were used as bomb shelters and could house as many as 35,000 people.

The visitor's tour is not a long one and you are given a map or can have a guide, but it takes you to the most interesting places and is well marked with letters and arrows. After passing beneath the road you ascend again by another staircase. This will lead you to the main gallery with its cannon chambers and loopholes which have been enlarged so that you can enjoy the views. Fifty cannons were once installed in this gallery.

Turning right you will find yourself in the cellars of the keep where again there is a lovely view from an enlarged loophole. At one time there were holes in the stone roof vaulting through which cannon could be lowered to save manhandling them up and down steps. An iron doorway then leads into a 'battery' which has four loopholes and used to house eight cannons, two to each loophole. This arrangement minimized the weakening of the fortification and enabled one of each pair to be fired while the other was withdrawn for muzzle loading.

Following the arrows you return upstairs through another gallery to the tower of the old castle labelled 'D' on the plan. Through the loophole here you see the remains of a fort on the far side of a ravine. To the right, on the top of the cliff, there is an old ruined tower known as the 'Hollow Tooth', a relic of Sigefroid's castle.

Go back to the main gallery and turn right towards letter 'E'. This marks the well of the former castle which is 150 feet deep. Return to the main gallery and the letter 'F' denotes the former headquarters of the 82-year-old Field Marshal von Bender during a siege in 1794-95. The one room served as bedroom, office and antechamber. From a loophole you look across inaccessible crags towards the old Spanish ramparts built in 1632. Below lies the city, the old Abbey of Munster, its church reflected in the waters of the Alzette, several aged towers and remnants of the third encircling wall. Again returning to the main gallery you can take a narrow passage to the right and, if you descend a staircase, you will pass beneath the 'Hollow Tooth' and then underneath a bridge. Loopholes to the left were used to protect the walls and the moat which was hollowed out between the castle and the Alzette river. On the right there is a chamber which used to house various guards and the letter 'G' denotes mine holes which were made ready in case of having to blow up part of the citadel. You return the same way you came and, if the above sounds complicated, the arrows and lettering are very simple to follow. If you suffer from claustrophobia you can always turn back but the views from the loopholes are exceptional.

Dramatic by day, the city presents an ethereal aspect after dark when much of it is floodlit. An old redoubt known as the Three Acorns is striking for each of its three towers is crowned with a giant ornamental acorn. One of the most intriguing little chapels I have ever seen can be glimpsed from the Passerelle bridge. It is far below in a cleft of rock on the south side of the ravine. Being very small it blends into the rock and parkland below so that it is easily missed. This Chapel of Saint Quirinus, hewn out of the solid rock in the fourth century, is one of the oldest shrines in Christendom. There is conjecture that the earliest worshippers' great grandparents there may have known one of the 12 disciples of Our Lord but there is no evidence to support this.

As has been mentioned before, music is an important part of every Luxembourger's life and in June there is a singing and instrumental music festival in the capital. Robert Schumann was born on the outskirts of the city at Clausen near the Three Acorn Towers, and it was in Luxembourg that Liszt gave his last recital in the Casino.

Famous writers and painters have also loved the city. Goethe was enchanted with the views in the capital and in his *Campaign in France* describes the ancient citadel as a place 'where so much grandeur and grace, sombre solemnity and exquisite loveliness are found side by side that one can only wish that Poussin, the remarkable French painter of the seventeenth century, had seen and painted it'.

If Poussin did not visit Luxembourg, Turner was to do so later when on one of his extensive European travels and he did several lovely watercolour sketches of the city.

We were fortunate enough to attend the unveiling of Luxembourg's memorial to Sir Winston Churchill on 23 October 1973. It is a statue of Sir Winston by the British sculptor, Oscar Nemon, who had known him well and has created several other figures of the former British Prime Minister. It had been commissioned under the patronage of Duke Jean by the *Association des Anciens Combattants,* The British-Luxembourg Society and the *Ligue des Prisonniers Politique et Déportés* – but that was not all. Men and women from all parts of the country made generous contributions for, as was pointed out at the inauguration by the President of the British-Luxembourg Society, René Schaaf, Sir Winston has a national significance for Luxembourg for his speeches rang out over occupied Europe louder than the guns and bombs of the enemy and entered the homes and the hearts of the subjected. 'In war : Resolution. In defeat : Defiance'.

When Colette Flesch, Lady Mayoress of Luxembourg city, spoke on this same occasion, she did it in a most unusual way by addressing Mr Churchill himself. She began, 'Once again you have come to Luxembourg', and continued to recall what an inspiration he had been to the Luxembourg people during the war years. How delighted everyone had been when he was made an honorary citizen and continued, 'since your first triumphal visit in our capital city, on the morrow of the Second World War, historians and biographers have laid claim upon your person, your life and your work'. At the end of her speech Mayoress Flesch bowed her head and said : 'Thank you for coming, Mr Churchill'.

Churchill had visited Luxembourg in July 1946 for the first time and was accompanied by his daughter Mary, now Lady Soames. Here, 27 years later she was to unveil his statue in the green square named after him.

Duke Jean, in uniform, had inspected a guard of honour of British troops who had come for the occasion from the British Army of the Rhine, a strange irony. The Duke then went back to a dais in front of a Grand Stand to join his mother, the Grand Duchess Charlotte, and his wife, who was holding a small bouquet of pale yellow roses which had been presented to her when she arrived and exactly matched her coat. The Diplomatic Corps and other dignitaries waited silently with members of the public while Lady Soames walked slowly towards a podium. She looked very attractive in a tailored strawberry coloured coat and a small black mink hat.

She recalled her visit with her father to Luxembourg and continued :

'The sun was shining; there were roses everywhere. The warmth of the reception given to him in the villages, in the towns and in the capital was overwhelming. And I had the privilege of witnessing this wonderful, unforgettable welcome, sitting next to you, Sir (with these words she turned towards Duke Jean with a smile) in the second car. I can remember my father's emotion and joy and my own feelings of pride to see him so received, as if it were yesterday.
My father spoke, at that time, of the "strong principle of

vitality, of personality, which has preserved the independent and sovereign life of the Grand Duchy of Luxembourg across so many centuries of shock and change and through the devastating cataclysm of the two last great European and World Wars".

Nor do we forget, Sir (another smile and nod to Duke Jean) that you yourself were an officer in the Irish Guards and that you played your part in the Liberation of Europe serving with The Guards Armoured Division. So the Royal House of Luxembourg and its people were equally an inspiration and an example to all those who were fighting in the cause of freedom and justice.

When Lady Soames had finished her speech she walked over to the draped statue and pulled the unveiling cord. Sir Winston is in a standing position with one foot forward as if to walk up the square. He holds his hat in his left hand and his chin is set determinedly, as if he is about to reply to Mayor Flesch's words.

Your presence amongst us, in the heart of this city, on a square which bears your name, will remind your contemporaries, your fellows at arms but also the young generations of the epic of the years 1940 to 1945. Your presence will more specifically call forth, for those who lived these dramatic hours, memories of your voice carried by the microphones of the BBC and lifting us out of the dismal resignation of the vanquished; a voice which, telling us that Britain was carrying on the struggle, gave us hope and confidence.

Churchill's visit to Luxembourg in July 1946 was followed by one of General Eisenhower in September of that year. Later, in 1952, he returned again during his farewell tour of Europe and visited General Patton's grave at Hamm Military Cemetery. There is now a memorial to General Patton at Ettelbruck where he had launched the counter-offensive, in December 1944, that turned the tide of the Battle of the Bulge. It is in the form of a square plinth surmounted by an American eagle with outspread wings. Close to it is a statue of the General in battle dress holding a pair of binoculars and near him there is an American tank of the Second World War.

Luxembourg has two popular hotels on the outskirts of the city, the luxurious Aerogolf with 150 rooms and the Holiday Inn with 203. In the city itself there are several smaller ones and the two where we have stayed are equally comfortable and both within walking distance of most places you would like to visit.

The Cravat, owned by the family 'Cravat', is an old establishment brought up to date but with large rooms and a delightful restaurant. The Hotel Central Molitor is not large and has small rooms but very well equipped. Each room has an electric door opener which you use from your bed in the morning when your breakfast arrives. Instead of the usual 'Do not disturb' cardboard signs to hang on the outside door knob you can use a luminous sign by pressing a button. The double-glazed windows, are easily opened which is unusual. There is a telephone in your bathroom and a wall safe in your bedroom. Again the restaurant is small but the menu is comprehensive and the specialities are Riesling meat pie, trout with almonds, mixed grill, veal scallop *cordon bleu,* pepper steak and cock stew with Riesling sauce.

The Holiday Inn is less than a mile from the centre of the city. It has plenty of parking space, is fully air-conditioned and has a heated pool and sauna. Its coffee shop is called 'The Bock' after the Citadel in Luxembourg city. There is a restaurant decorated in rustic style. One of its specialities is an appetising cold buffet. During the evening there is a piano player in the bar. Trolleys are provided to ferry your luggage from your car to your room if no porter is available.

The modern Aerogolf Hotel, as its name suggests, is near the airport and opposite an 18-hole golf course, ideal for a flying golf weekend. The hotel operates its own courtesy bus service assuring regular connections with both the city and the airport. In spite of its proximity, aircraft noise really is eliminated by treble-glazing. The hotel is the brainchild of M Alphonse Theisen the managing director of the company which owns it. Elegantly furnished throughout, the pleasant foyer lounge features comfortable black leather seating. There are two bars, 'The Green' on the ground floor and 'The Cockpit' on the top. The restaurant and grill room are both delightful and overlook an extensive garden and woods.

There are regular flights by Luxair, British Airways and Northeast Airlines from the United Kingdom to the airport which is only about three miles from Luxembourg city by motorway. Icelandic Airways and Loftleidir/International Air Bahamas, the latter not bound by the IATA fare convention, also have their European terminal here.

3. Places to Visit in Luxembourg

In such a small country as Luxembourg you can make the capital your base if you wish to avoid packing and unpacking, although there are numerous very good hotels around the countryside. It is a matter of personal taste but the following visits can be made within a day's drive out and back to the city. If you do not have your car there is an elaborate network of bus and railway lines covering the country. You can buy one- and five-day tickets from Luxembourg Rail, which includes bus travel also. Services to most parts of the country run about hourly throughout the day. During the summer season you can go by boat along the scenic route between Schengen and Wasserbillig.

Vianden, one of the most beautiful towns in the Luxembourg Ardennes, lies in the northern section of the country. To whet your appetite I can do no better than quote an unknown writer who, like Victor Hugo, fell in love with it.

. . . If I had to see only one castle, one landscape and one town, it is Vianden that I would choose. It is at one and the same time the most elaborate and wildest spot to be seen on this side of the Rhine. The castle is enormous; it is one with the rock, then draws its towers away to rear them toward heaven. At its feet, the village tumbles down the slopes in little medieval streets. Here nothing has changed since the times when Victor Hugo, a voluntary exile, came here to meditate and dream in a framework worthy of his genius.

You leave the capital by route 7 and make your way to Diekirch, some 20 miles distant, a little town of 5,000 inhabitants on the tree-lined River Sûre at the foot of the Herrenberg. The town is famous for its beer which you can sample if you visit the brewery. It was at Diekirch that I drank my first glass of the 'new' wine which was most refreshing to the taste, rather like unsweetened grapefruit juice. However, it has a very high alcoholic content, so it is wise not to indulge too freely. It is served by the glass in cafés and inns for about three weeks each autumn after the grape gathering.

Diekirch has much to offer: numerous walks through lovely parkland and by the river; beech trees grow along the hills and its small conical towered church dates back to the twelfth century. On the outskirts of the town is the 'Devil's Altar', a Celtic dolmen, probably a sacrificial stone in olden times.

Vianden is about 30 miles from the capital. For the last mile or so the road winds downward and a truly glorious view opens up as you descend into a beautiful valley across which you can see the 1,000-year-old castle of Vianden perched, like an eagle's eyrie, on a high hilltop. It is one of the largest feudal fortresses on the continent. The size and importance of this castle in its prime may be gauged from the fact that the Knight's Hall could accommodate 500 men-at-arms. A curious feature of the chapel is an hexagonal hole in the centre of the floor, opening into a bare subterranean dungeon. Originally this may have been copied from the 'double chapel' of the Church of the Holy Sepulchre in Jerusalem. It was built by Count Frederick II on his return from the crusades.

Vianden possesses one of the oldest charters in Europe, granted in the fourteenth century by Philip, Count of Vianden, from whom the family of Nassau-Vianden sprang, and who was consequently an ancestor of William of Orange. The semi-mythical founder of this family was Bertha, the 'White Lady', who figures in many German legends. By family connection Vianden Castle is the ancestral home of Duke Jean and also of Queen Juliana of Holland, whose ancestor Otho married Adelaide of Vianden in 1350. Other hills encircle this attractive town and a chairlift rises to a vantage point whence truly theatrical views can be enjoyed. Against this magnificent backdrop Vianden Castle stands out with its corbelled turrets, gables and ramparts. During the summer its fairy-tale appearance is further enhanced by illumination after dark and on a clear moonlit night it seems to float in space.

Vianden's Gothic church, with its two naves, was built in 1248 and is one of the oldest religious buildings in Luxembourg. The museum has some fine antique furniture and the small house once owned by Victor Hugo is also open as a museum.

Victor Joly wrote a book called *The Ardennes* in 1857 which Victor Hugo had read and he fell in love with the idea of Vianden. He visited the town several times. To his romantic mind it left nothing to be desired and he described it as a 'Splendid landscape which one day all Europe will visit'. He chose it as a refuge during part of his exile from France, and bought a little house near the bridge at the edge of the town. The contents of the house are original as they were hidden during the Second World War, but the house itself was demolished and had to be rebuilt. Engravings, yellowing photographs and letters decorate the walls and show facets of Hugo's life with his friends. There are also sketches which he made of Vianden.

Upstairs there is his small bedroom and study with a hard-backed chair and a plain desk beneath a window overlooking the bridge and street below. It was here that he wrote one of his finest works *L'Année Terrible,* illustrating the suffering of Paris during the siege.

Victor Hugo takes his place in French literature alongside Shakespeare in England and Goethe in Germany; like them, he enjoyed working in congenial surroundings. He used to fling open his study window on sunny days and seek inspiration from the lines of trees on the hilltops or gaze down at the river into the rushing waters of the Our. In the same way as the figure of Shakespeare broods over the river Avon in Stratford, the bust of Hugo, hair tousled, forehead wrinkled with thought, ponders near the bridge over the river Our.

In the neighbourhood of Vianden are more ruined castles, notably those of Stalzemburg and Brandenbourg. Although Vianden maintains its medieval character and its historic monuments, these do not shut it off from technical progress. Indeed it has one of the most powerful hydro-electric pumped storage plants in the world, which you must visit if time allows, for it is an instance where man's ever-increasing demand for energy has been met with improvement to rather than degradation of the environment. Artificial lakes have been created which blend perfectly into the scenery of the Our valley and make your visit to them really worthwhile even if you have no interest in mechanical things. The generating plant is concealed in giant halls hewn out of rock and so does not obtrude.

In essence the scheme is a vast accumulator storing energy at night when spare generating capacity elsewhere makes it cheap, and feeding it back into the system, much of it to German industry, during the daytime when demand is heavy. The principle is simple and there are now a number of installations throughout the world, though that at Vianden was one of the first. During off-peak periods enormous pumps draw water from reservoirs in the Our valley and pump it into other reservoirs on the top of Mont Saint Nicolas. When the demand for electric energy rises these same pumps become hydro-electric generators and the water in the upper lakes flows back through them into the valley lake again.

To go into the underground visitor's gallery overlooking the vast subterranean turbine hall is reminiscent of a visit to another world. Working diagrams making the intriguing operation of the installation easy to understand and quoted figures give an idea of the vast scale of the enterprise.

As opposed to artificial lakes there are natural thermal springs in the extreme south east of the Grand Duchy at Mondorf-les-Bains in yet another charming valley, that of the Gander. It is only 11 miles from Luxembourg city and is on the frontier with

France. The casino park is handsomely landscaped and has a small lake for boating. There are several hotels and pensions open from April until October and during the season there are all kinds of sports and recreations. It is claimed that the spring waters contain chlorides, sulphates and alkalis with a trace of radium. Liver, heart and blood ailments are treated. There are some very good restaurants and, if you enjoy grills, the 'Hotel du Grand Chef' specializes in them. Walks in the countryside around Mandorf are rewarding with picturesque views out over the Moselle valley a couple of miles away.

Luxembourg is honeycombed with walking tracks and these are marked and signposted so that you know what distance you will cover. It is a great pastime to leave your car and follow one of the circular walking tours which will eventually bring you back to your vehicle. In each district the tourist bureau will give you information and supply maps or mark your own for you. Wooded tracks will lead you to waterfalls, prehistoric caves and grottoes, past castles and through delightful scenery. Although walking is so popular you seldom meet many people.

The Moselle valley is famed for its wine and grape festivals. Route 1 out of Luxembourg city joins with Route 10 at Greven-macher, which is one of the wine centres where you can stop to visit the well known caves of Bernard-Massard or the Coopera-tive of Vinegrowers' Cellars.

Another route to the vineyard region is to drive along the European highway E42 which passes through small grape grow-ing districts stretched along the Moselle river like a row of beads. Indeed Remich is known as the 'Pearl of Luxembourg's Moselle'. These little towns are reached along a pretty roadway with the slow-moving river on one side and on the other innumerable terraces reaching up the hillsides. Vines have grown on these hills since Roman colonists first planted them and poets have praised the wine they produced. Ausonius in his *Moselle* describes the river as 'the pleasant stream . . . whose hills are overgrown with Bacchus' fragrant vines'. Fortunatus thought highly of the light, dry wines of the district.

At Remich little pleasure boats wait for customers along an embankment overhung with willows behind which stretches a promenade. Fishermen try their luck and nearby is a memorial in the form of an anchor. The base of the tower in the old town wall is surrounded with potted plants. The ancient gateway, Porte Saint Nicolas, its archway festooned with trailing greenery, leads through to narrow little streets. It is a peaceful, quiet place and the wine cellars Caves Saint Martin are open to visitors.

My favourite little town along the river is Ehnen, really a village of some 250 inhabitants where everyone seems to be concerned with the production of wine. I first visited it after the grape harvest and the smell of fermentation was in the air. Each little grey stone house had its half-underground cellar doors ajar and along the pavements several large wooden troughs were drying in the sun. Neat flower pots edged the sills behind each window. This charming little village has the only circular church in the country and it is dedicated to Saint Nicolas. It is snow-white with a stone tower to one side. The church is about 60 feet in diameter with a domed roof and a skylight in the centre. 'Round' churches were built in the Middle Ages not only as places of worship but for defence as well. The only examples I had seen before were in Denmark on the island of Bornholm where there are four. The Danish ones were also painted white and were built in the twelfth century. Their beehive shapes are most appealing with decorated belfries.

The Eisch valley, called the Valley of the Seven Castles, is one of the most picturesque drives in the country. You leave by route E9 westward to the beginning of the valley of Steinfort. There are camping grounds and over 40 miles of marked walking tracks. Some of these lead you round in a circle so you can get back to your car. There are also hotels, inns, cafés and restaurants to suit all pockets. Route E9 continues to Korich where there are the ruins of the first castle, Grevenschloss. Only a few walls of this 1585 edifice stand today but there is an interesting seventeenth-century church with an onion-shaped tower surmounted by an open belfry. The next castle, Septfontaines, sits on a hilltop above a small village and dates back to the thirteenth century. The seven fountains around the base of the hill gave it is name.

The road then continues to Ansembourg where there are two castles – a fairly new one in the valley and the ruins of an ancient one on a hilltop. The monastery of the order of White Fathers is in Marienthal. As is suggested by their name they wear long white robes and undertake missionary work in Africa and the Middle East. They have a little museum with relics from the various countries in which they have worked.

The Castle of Hollenfels has been restored and is now a youth hostel. Its church nearby has also been repaired and over the entrance, standing in a niche, is a knight in full armour who invariably attracts photographers.

The castle at Mersch is an early feudal one. The modern little town is the crossroads of tourist routes in the centre of the country. Its historical buildings are illuminated at night during the season. It has the remains of a Roman villa with mosaics. A village nearby has the quaint name of Angel's Hill – Angelsberg.

Clervaux Castle is not in the same valley but is further north in the Ardennes. This impressive castle once belonged to the de Lannoi family. Much of it was destroyed in 1944 but it has since been restored. It houses many beautiful models of the most important castles in the country.

Wiltz Castle has American connections and here the town offers something unique. Part surrounds the castle to form the upper town while the remainder lies some 500 feet below. As you traverse the lacets from one part to the other you will pass yet another Second World War tank preserved as a memorial. Every summer theatrical productions are staged in the castle grounds with the castle itself as a backdrop. It also contains the 'Battle of the Bulge' museum which will be of interest to many visitors. Uniforms, helmets, rifles and other reminders are cleverly displayed. You enter and leave through curtains of camouflage netting which give the right atmosphere.

Of the towns in Luxembourg that of Echternach some 14 miles from the capital is perhaps one of the most interesting and it has a particular link with Britain because Saint Willibrord, the Anglo-Saxon monk from Northumberland who brought Christianity to Northern Europe, founded the famous Benedictine Abbey there.

You leave from Luxembourg north east along Route E42 going through Junglinster where you can see six masts of Radio Luxembourg some 750 feet high. Continuing along route E42 right to the town takes you through part of Luxembourg's 'Little Switzerland'. Echternach is in a lush valley of fields, meadows, orchards and vineyards and is on the right bank of the river Sauer.

The most outstanding place in the town is the enormous abbey, part of which is a school for boys and girls. There are seven grammar schools in Luxembourg and this one serves the northern part of the country. It was begun as a small monastery in AD 698 by Willibrord for Christian missionaries travelling through the country and he later added an almshouse, both being built on land given by Princess Irmina. When her parents died Willibrord was given their great estates and in AD 705 the territory was further enlarged by a vast donation of land from another rich benefactor, Pepin d'Herustal. Gradually the abbey and its many buildings grew into a self-contained town with its own ramparts and Willibrord's feudal rights were bequeathed to his successors. Later the abbots became known as 'Lords of Echternach'. Nothing much remains of the original buildings today but the abbey's size and importance during the Middle Ages and up to the time of the French Revolution was such that it was renowned throughout Europe. At the time of the Germanic Federation in 1843, 500 Luxembourg soldiers were quartered in one wing of the abbey.

Every Whit Tuesday the memory of Saint Willibrord, who is also a patron saint of fountains and springs, is honoured by a strange dance, a most curious religious celebration. It begins about 9 o'clock in the morning. The tolling of a seven-ton church bell is the signal to start the procession, which is accompanied by bands and singers. Traditionally pilgrims hop some five steps forward and three backward. The distance covered by the dancers is not far yet the procession lasts most of the day. The dancers hop up and down to music repeated over and over again, each person gripping a twisted white handkerchief with his or her neighbour. Four or more abreast, old and young, they veer to the left and then to the right, gradually moving through the narrow winding streets to the town square. Here they turn towards the basilica, dance down the aisle, are blessed by the clergy and emerge again to disperse. The rest of the day is spent in merrymaking, feasting and drinking Moselle wines.

No one seems to know how the idea of this procession started. One legend has it that a man named Guy went to the Holy Land to seek forgiveness for a crime. He is said to have murdered his wife. When he returned to Echternach he was sentenced to be hanged although he had confessed his crime and it was felt that God had forgiven him. As a last request he asked to be allowed to play a lute. He played so beautifully that people began to dance. When Willibrord saw that the populace were happy he blessed their dancing and the condemned man was pardoned and vanished from sight. The expression in French 'Dance de Saint Guy' is sometimes used for epileptic fits.

The same background of epilepsy is the keynote of another legend. In the seventh century some local people were afflicted with Saint Vitus's Dance and again Saint Willibrord came to the rescue. 'Do penance, pray and accept Christianity and the illness will go', he promised. Penance meant some kind of physical punishment and so, to the jaunty tune that is still played today and is said to be an Irish jig, the people hopped up and down until exhausted. Almost overnight, it is said, those who had epileptic fits recovered their normal health and accepted Christianity.

The Whit Tuesday dance celebrations have only been forbidden on two occasions: once by Napoleon and once in 1940 though, even then, it was allowed for a small group. Thousands of visitors and Roman Catholics from many countries come for the event each year, either to join in or to watch. 'Holy Willibrord, founder of churches, light of the blind, destroyer of idols, pray for us', is chanted over and over again. Miraculous cures are sometimes attributed to this act of devotion.

The Basilica of Saint Willibrord was severely damaged during the Second World War but fortunately the crypt was not affected. The latter has served many purposes through the centuries; as a burial place for monks, a treasury and even at times as a prison. It was one of the Merovingian churches of the seventh century mentioned in the title deeds of Princess Irmina who was made a saint after her death. The subterranean church is one of the oldest Christian sanctuaries in the country. Recent repair work uncovered several remarkable frescoes of the eleventh century depicting scenes of the Virgin Mary's life.

Saint Willibrord is said to have been buried under the altar of the first church in 739. His remains were then placed under a new high altar when the third abbey church was consecrated in 1031. During the French Revolution the Saint's relics were scattered but were later placed in a sarcophagus in the local Church of Saint Peter and Saint Paul. They were transferred back to the basilica in 1906 and you can visit the tomb in the crypt. A vault, protected by a wrought iron gate, now contains the tomb. At last his bones have found a resting place and are enshrined in a Carrara marble sarcophagus.

Within the walls of the abbey is the Garden of Prelates. Designed in the French style its walks, lined with mythological statues, lead up to an orangery whose façade is decorated with statues representing the four seasons.

The abbey park stretches along the river Sauer with a delightful pavilion in Rococo style. From the pavilion terrace or walking along the river bank one can watch leaping trout in the rushing water, and see on the far bank of the river (which is Germany) the woods which contain the remains of the Siegfried line fortifications of the Second World War.

Echternach was the pivot of von Rundstedt's last great push

and became no-man's-land from October 1944 to March 1945. Both the Germans and Americans were there during that time. Patton's army was short of petrol and so had to stay there. The Germans had left their Siegfried line fortresses but returned when the Americans did not pursue them. Then fighting raged over the town while the Americans tried to cross the Sauer by temporary bridging but they had very heavy losses. Indeed during the ensuing battles the town was completely razed and the magnificent abbey left in ruins.

It has been entirely rebuilt and the town square has been reconstructed exactly as it was before. This was accomplished in three years and much of the credit must go to Echternach's remarkable Burgomaster, Robert Schaffner. He went through ghastly experiences in such concentration camps as Buchenwald during the war but his story has an unusually happy ending and epitomises the spirit of Luxembourg.

Robert Schaffner, a boy scout at the age of 11 years and today the only scout in Luxembourg besides Grand Duke Jean to have been awarded the Silver Wolf, was a blacksmith before the war. He was sent to a concentration camp in Germany in 1942. By a stroke of luck the camp sergeant did not particularly dislike Luxembourgers and on one occasion took Robert to a workshop where there was a radio so that he could listen to Grand Duchess Charlotte speaking from England. The sergeant himself actually stood guard outside the workshop while the speech was being broadcast. Later Robert Schaffner was sent to Buchenwald. His fellow prisoners there were Czechs, Poles, French and Belgians. His facility for languages enabled him to act as a liaison officer between the different resistance groups in the camp because there was a hard fight for supremacy going on. The guards were Germans, whom the others called the 'Greens', and they were without exception criminals let out of prison for this purpose. They killed many of those in the camp resistance groups and in turn some of them were murdered. The 'Greens' job was to destroy the morale of anyone wearing a red triangle, the sign of a political prisoner. The ss outside the camp confiscated most of the meagre rations meant for the prisoners and sold them on the black market. Schnapps and tobacco were like gold both outside and inside the camp.

Life was unbearable and was no better when Robert was sent to Lublin. His undercover work continued and he was threatened with extermination. One of the guards who was a driver slipped him a little food and tobacco now and then and this he used for bargaining purposes. Then he had a third piece of luck. It was known from his papers that he was a blacksmith and mechanically minded and one of the guards had an aged lorry which had broken down and could not be repaired. He was in despair about this and Robert's contact, the other guard, suggested that he should bring Robert along to try and mend the lorry. This Robert did and taught the eldest son of the owner, a lad of nearly 17, how to overhaul the lorry and maintain it properly. This took time and gave a spark of hope for the future. However it was short-lived. Robert was moved again, this time to the Auschwitz camp. His wife and child were also prisoners in Silesia and he had not heard from them for months. Suddenly, it seemed to those in the concentration camps, the war ended just as quickly as it had begun.

The first news of peace Robert got was when he was moved yet again. This time to Gross-Rosen and finally Leitmeritz in Silesia. At last the emaciated prisoners were free although cholera and typhus were still enemies. Robert joined up with three American soldiers and two Frenchmen and they managed to purloin a car and drove to Prague. From there the Americans got them by Red Cross car to Pilsen and then by jeep to Wurzburg. There Canadians arranged for the men to go their separate ways and Robert eventually got back to Luxembourg. He was weak after nearly fours years of diabolical treatment and had only three thoughts in his mind; to find his wife and child, to return to Echternach and to repay the three men who had given him a gleam of hope during the years of war. He achieved all three ambitions.

When he first returned home Robert was so ill that he was

taken to five different doctors who all suggested different treatment. He ignored all the advice and miraculously, his wife and child returned to Echternach within 28 days of his own arrival. They had been hidden initially for over a year and a half in the Black Forest and Robert added a fourth ambition : to repay the family who had sheltered his wife and child for so long.

Robert Schaffner began at the beginning. He traced the ss camp sergeant who had allowed him to hear Grand Duchess Charlotte's speech. The man had at one time been in British, American and French prison camps and Robert managed to secure his freedom.

On Saint George's Day 1946, Robert, in his capacity as Luxembourg's Chief Scout, was presented with a medal by King George at Windsor Castle. He took part in the divine service at Saint George's Chapel and the parade that followed. During the reception afterwards he was asked to talk about his wartime experiences to the King and Queen. How interesting it would be to know what he said but when I asked him he smiled : 'It was a very pleasant occasion!'

A German pow heard about the celebrations at Windsor that day. He was the German guard who had slipped Robert a little food and tobacco so long ago. He was freed. The owner of the lorry was tracked down, also a pow, and again Robert managed to pry him loose; lastly the family which had been so kind to Robert's wife and daughter.

The commandant of the French pow camp where the man was held had been at Saint Cyr with the Mayor of Luxembourg City, a close friend of Robert's, so again it was not long before he too was reunited with his family in the Schwartzwald.

I have not related Robert Schaffner's story exactly as he told me and certainly I had to leave out many interesting and distressing episodes. However, I have recounted it in some detail for several reasons. It is not often that such an unpleasant ordeal ends so happily and affords the opportunity to repay the human kindness encountered. It is given to few men to achieve the ideal of rebuilding their home town after a major disaster. Many men are not tough enough to withstand the privation of prison camps and certainly afterwards would lack the determination needed to direct major civic projects. Lastly, in some way the Robert Schaffner story typifies the Luxembourgers' motto – 'We wish to remain what we are'.

Index

LUXEMBOURG